T0076881

WHEN THE
GRID FAILS

WHEN THE GRID FAILS: EASY ACTION STEPS WHEN FACING URBAN AND NATURAL DISASTERS

Copyright © 2022 by Cider Mill Press Book Publishers LLC.

This is an officially licensed book by Cider Mill Press Book Publishers LLC.
All rights reserved under the Pan-American and International Copyright Conventions.

No part of this book may be reproduced in whole or in part, scanned, photocopied, recorded, distributed in any printed or electronic form, or reproduced in any manner whatsoever, or by any information storage and retrieval system now known or hereafter invented, without express written permission of the publisher, except in the case of brief quotations embodied in critical articles and reviews.

The scanning, uploading, and distribution of this book via the internet or via any other means without permission of the publisher is illegal and punishable by law. Please support authors' rights, and do not participate in or encourage piracy of copyrighted materials.

13-Digit ISBN: 978-1-64643-253-0
10-Digit ISBN: 1-64643-253-3

This book may be ordered by mail from the publisher. Please include $5.99 for postage and handling. Please support your local bookseller first!

Books published by Cider Mill Press Book Publishers are available at special discounts for bulk purchases in the United States by corporations, institutions, and other organizations. For more information, please contact the publisher.

Cider Mill Press Book Publishers
"Where good books are ready for press"
501 Nelson Place
Nashville, Tennessee 37214

cidermillpress.com

Typography: Interstate, Yorkten Slab

Image credits: Pages 15-16, 19, 21, 31, 40-41, 50, 61, 76, 80-81, 82, 85, 89, 92, 97, 99, 109, 111, 127, 194-195, 199, 201 (bottom right), 202-203, 210, 213, 227, 231, 248-249 used under official license from Shutterstock.com

All other images courtesy of Cider Mill Press.

Printed in Malaysia

23 24 25 26 27 TJM 6 5 4 3 2

WHEN THE GRID FAILS

EASY ACTION STEPS WHEN FACING URBAN AND NATURAL DISASTERS

BY KY FURNEAUX

CIDER MILL
PRESS

BOOK
PUBLISHERS

Contents

Introduction

The Attitude
of Survival

I EXPLORE MY ENVIRONMENT AND EXPERIMENT with survival skills at every opportunity, and as a result, my approach to survival is slightly different from the traditional ways of looking at it. Survival has been thought of as a scenario that requires the biggest, strongest, and most skilled person to make it through, and also requires certain gear to make your time in the emergency survivable. And if you don't have that strength and gear, then you might as well curl up and die. I don't believe that and have fought against those opinions for years. I believe that anyone can survive with the right mindset and attitude.

Will knowledge help get you through? Absolutely, if applied with the right attitude. Will being prepared with the right gear help get you through? Definitely. But nine times out of ten, we aren't expecting to be put in a survival situation, which is why it becomes a life-or-death struggle.

This book equips you with knowledge that will help you survive and endure any number of unexpected natural and urban disasters. But first you need to prepare your mindset. I will provide you with ways of looking at your specific situation that will have you understanding what your priorities are and how best to deal with them.

This book isn't about instilling fear in you about all the possible horrible things that could happen to you in this world. Quite the opposite, actually. I want you to know that whatever unexpected event happens, with the right mindset, a bit of preparation, and some general knowledge, you have a good chance of making it out the other side of a disaster with merely some memorable stories to show for it.

I want you to become flexible with your thinking—sometimes trying to remember and follow a rigid set of rules will be more detrimental to you than observing what is going on in the moment and finding your best mode of moving through the situation. I will teach you the properties of assets to look for, rather than specific resources, and I'll explain the theories behind what works and why, rather than giving you endless methods to memorize.

I want to empower you to know the difference between your wants and your needs and focus on what you can change rather than obsessing over what you can't.

I want you to understand why some people give up in a survival scenario and why others manage to beat the odds, in the hope that you can train your mindset to get you through any range of unexpected circumstances.

Above all, I want you to learn to be proactive in doing what you need to do in your specific scenario to keep you and your loved ones safe and alive.

No matter the circumstances, the following tips are essential to being in the right mindset to get through a survival situation:

BE POSITIVE

How often do we hear this saying? It comes out of the mouth of every single motivational speaker I've ever heard. Be positive. It's a catchphrase that people often throw at you without a thought for telling you how to be positive when times are tough. But it is a popular phrase for a reason. It really can turn your life and a situation around, and becoming negative has been proven to hasten someone toward giving up, especially in a dire scenario.

ACKNOWLEDGE THE SITUATION

The first thing I do when I have found myself in a less-than-ideal situation is to acknowledge it. Imagine that your plane has crashed, and you are the only survivor. That's an awful situation to be in. Denial of a situation is a short-term solution and often ends badly when reality sets in, so it is important to take a realistic look at what has happened and where you are. Unfortunately, this is where most people then sit and dwell, but this is where you need to move on from.

Choosing to be negative about the situation you are in brings the focus onto, and enhances the perception of, the bad things about the circumstances. If you are in a survival situation, you may be cold, tired, and hungry, but focusing on those things will not make them go away. By concentrating on them, you can make them seem worse than they are. Choose instead to focus on what you do have, like the fact that you are alive and coherent.

Looking at the things that are working for you will help you figure out how best to deal with the situation. It will allow you to discover your strengths and then use them to your advantage.

ASSESS YOUR ASSETS

Take stock of what is working for you in the situation: Are you injured? Can you function? What resources do you have? Do you know where you are? The more things that you can find that are in your favor, the less you will focus on the dire scenario. There is a difference between focusing on the negatives and assessing your weaknesses.

Focusing on the negatives is complaining that you are hot. Assessing your weaknesses is realizing that you are sitting in a desert with a broken-down car, no water, and no service on your phone. Noting these weaknesses will allow you to make a strategy and act.

KNOW THE DIFFERENCE BETWEEN A WANT AND A NEED

A need is something that will cause you to die if you don't have it. A want is everything else. I was once on a television show with another person where we were placed in an extreme survival situation. He spent a lot of time focusing on things that he wanted that we were never going to be able to get access to, like hamburgers and pancakes. His constant chatter about these things kept me focused on the lack we had in the situation. I did much better mentally if I focused on what we had around us and satisfied my basic needs, rather than wishing for the impossible.

I think the Serenity Prayer says it best when it talks about having the strength to do without the things you can't have, the courage to fight for the things you can have, and the knowledge to know the difference between the two. At least that's my interpretation of it, anyway.

BE PRODUCTIVE

A question I ask myself when I am in extreme survival scenarios is "What can I do today to make tomorrow better?" Not only does it help me improve my current conditions, but it keeps me proactive and in success mode. The problem-solving aspect of the question keeps my mind from wandering to dark places and distracts me from focusing on what I don't have.

THIS TOO SHALL PASS

I have used this saying to get me through all sorts of situations where I have felt discomfort or pain, or faced something challenging, ranging from getting through a particularly hard workout in the gym to being so cold that I thought my toes were going to need to be amputated at the end of an expedition.

The thing to remember about discomfort is that, in most cases, it is only temporary. If you are cold, there are things you can do to become warmer. If you are overheating, there are things you can do to cool down. This saying is not a passive statement, however. It is a recognition of a situation and a starting point from which your actions can make the discomfort or danger pass and lead to a more positive mindset.

TAKE ACTION

From the second you realize things are looking grim, begin to do what you can to assist your survival and improve your situation. Not only will this increase the chances of making it out alive, but it will also enable you to be in better condition when you finally do get out. So once your plan is in place, take action.

- Whether you can read a topographic map instead of relying on the GPS

- Whether you have taken a first aid course at any point

- Whether you know methods of purifying water

PROPER PLANNING PREVENTS POOR PERFORMANCE (OR UNDESIRED OUTCOME)

Always make a plan. By weighing the pros and cons of the situation you are in, you will be able to find the best course of action. By making a plan, you will avoid wasting time and energy trying avenues of action that will not be effective. It may seem that taking the time to plan delays action and therefore prolongs an outcome. This may be the case sometimes (like when you need to move fast to avoid an oncoming obstacle), but usually sitting down and planning saves time in the long run. Taking time to make a plan will make you will feel proactive. In a survival situation, a feeling of help-lessness can be just as deadly as the environment you are in.

Your plan should assess the seriousness of the current situation. Was it an earthquake that shook your house for a few minutes? Did your fight-or-flight mechanism take you to the street, where you joined your neighbors for a quick chat, and then you were able to return to your home, straighten the pictures, and all was okay? Was it a hurricane that has left you without power and cut you off from the nearest town for three days? In that case, you will need to be thinking about how to keep yourself warm, hydrated, and fed until power can be reestablished.

Your plan should take into consideration your personal "tool kit." This is composed of the lessons and skills that you have learned through life, like the examples on page 12. The more education and skills that you bring into whatever situation life throws your way, the better your chance of coming out the other side with a positive result.

CHECK FOR YOURSELF

The "experts," including me, might not have all the answers. Don't assume that because someone has told you they can do something that they can actually do it, or that if something doesn't work, that it doesn't. I personally have debunked many survival "facts" presented to me as absolutes. And things that I have never managed to make work, I have seen others succeed in.

Your attitude in a survival scenario has a huge effect on the outcome of your situation. Only you can control your attitude, but the key is knowing that you can change it for the better and begin to take the steps toward ensuring your survival.

1

Natural Disasters

ACCIDENTS OR HUMAN ERROR are not the only ways you could end up in a life-or-death struggle. Natural disasters cause great damage or loss of human life. They can produce emergency scenarios that will demand the same survival attitudes and techniques you would use when lost in the woods. Disasters can happen anywhere and at any time, whether you are in remote locations or close to home.

Natural disasters occur all of the time all around the world, year after year. These disasters result in tens of thousands of deaths per year. Hundreds of millions of people are affected, whether through injury, loss, or damages. While the events themselves may not be preventable, the deaths and damage can be drastically reduced through:

- Early prediction

- Emergency preparedness

- Good response systems

Your first seconds, minutes, and hours count, and they can set you up for success or struggle.

The most important thing you can do in the first few minutes of a disaster is to stay calm. This may feel impossible to do as chaos reigns around you, but it will ensure a better outcome.

REMOVE YOURSELF FROM HARM'S WAY

If a car is coming toward you, get out of its path. If an earthquake is happening, get down low and take cover under something solid. If a tornado warning is sounding, head for the nearest storm shelter or safe room.

ASSESS YOUR CONDITION

Always remember that you will be no help to anyone if you haven't first taken care of yourself. It's the whole airplane strategy of making sure that you put your oxygen mask on before helping others. Are you injured? How badly? Can you fix it yourself? Do you need medical help? If you do need urgent attention, see to that first before assisting others.

The next appropriate response to a disaster is going to depend on what disaster you are facing. This is where the survival attitude of being adaptable becomes critical. It will be up to you to make the crucial decisions in the moment. I can't give you the answers to every possible scenario, but I can give you some steps to follow so that you will be able to make more educated and informed decisions.

People spend too much time dwelling on the fact the disaster has happened. Take a second to acknowledge the disaster; then move from seeing that it is happening to figuring out what you can do about it. Survival is largely about seeing a problem and finding a solution as quickly as possible.

ACTION PLAN

If you are okay, then your next priorities are as follows:

1. Stop to assess the situation. Some things to consider are:

- **Where are your loved ones?** Is it safe to get to them? If so, how?

- **Can you help others, or will it endanger you?** How do you judge what is dangerous? Look for immediate and obvious threats, such as downed power lines, swift-flowing water, thick smoke, increased agitation, or armed attackers. You will need to use common sense and err on the side of caution, if your survival comes down to it.

- **What are authorities saying?** How can you even gather information if the electricity and Wi-Fi are down? If the situation is serious enough, authorities will be making their presence and wishes felt with door-to-door evacuations.

- **What is the mood of the people around you?** Are tensions high, or are people banding together to help?

- **Is the danger over or just beginning?**

2. Make your location safe, or move to a safe place.

- **Check to see if it's structurally sound**

- **Have the ability to survey your surroundings**

- **Know your best evacuation path, and always have a plan B**

- **Be able to fortify the area to prevent undesirable entry**

- **Regulate temperature and access critical survival needs**

3. Once you have reached a safe place, and you have decided to hunker down, do an emergency needs assessment, which includes an inventory of the following:

- **Food**

- **Shelter**

- **Safe drinking water**

- **Total access to water, including containers for storage and carrying**

- **Essential items to moderate temperature, such as blankets and extra warm clothing**

- **Sanitation and waste disposal**

- **Medication and medical care, including a first aid kit**

- **Psychosocial support (entertainment and communication)**

4. Figure out how to improve your situation without compromising your safety, to turn your weaknesses or shortfalls into assets or strengths. Being proactive can stave off panic and a feeling of helplessness.

PANIC IS YOUR ENEMY

The first thing to remember about panic is that it can escalate a situation and spread to those around you.

Panic causes many symptoms, including a rapid heart rate and shortness of breath or tightness in your throat. Simply pausing and taking a few deep breaths can dramatically calm your nervous system and reduce these symptoms, leading to a reduction in the feeling of panic. Finding purpose can also reduce the feeling of panic, so either taking charge of the situation or finding tasks to assist in making the situation better eases this fear of impending doom.

Your calmness and take-charge attitude will spread, allowing the people around you to find a greater sense of calm as well. Speak firmly where needed, assign tasks even if they seem to be impractical, and listen to people's fears to address and alleviate them.

BE PREPARED

While some natural disasters can come out of nowhere, some destinations will experience certain types of disasters more often than others. Wildfires are the most common type of natural disasters, closely followed by floods. Research the history of natural disasters in your area, and take steps to prevent and prepare for them in and around your home. Make a go bag that can be filled with everything you need to survive an emergency, along with the things that you would be devastated to lose (see page 22). Have an action plan, and make sure all your loved ones know the plan, should the worst happen.

THE AFTERMATH

Sometimes the aftermath of a natural disaster can be worse than the actual disaster itself, as it can have wide-ranging and long-term consequences on infrastructure and ecosystems. You should be prepared to be able to survive independently for at least three days after a natural disaster. Chapter 2, Urban Survival, will address how to survive an extended scenario in your own home.

There is a saying that natural disasters happen when hazards meet vulnerabilities. The aim of the next section of *Survive* is to decrease your vulnerabilities so that you won't become another casualty that could have been avoided.

1.1

▶ GO BAG

A go bag, or bug out bag, is one of the more fiercely debated and personal methods of preparation for an emergency. For every "survival expert" on-line, there will be a different suggestion for how best to pack one and what it should contain. For me personally, I have a go bag packed with the idea that it will sustain me for an indefinite amount of time, should the worst come to be. This means that it needs to provide me with the ability to cover my basic survival needs of food, fire, water, and shelter for an extended pe-riod and assist me with rescue. The items need to be reusable and sustain-ing, rather than single use and disposable. It does mean that the contents of my bag require some level of education and skill to use, but I don't ever put anything in my go bag without knowing how to use it.

My go bag is specifically designed for a zombie-like apocalypse event where all of civilization has collapsed, but your go bag doesn't need to reflect such extremes. If you are in an urban environment where your greatest fear may be a bushfire, then your bag could contain precious, irreplaceable items and a few changes of underwear, should you need to flee your house for a few days. Ask yourself: What would I grab first if a fireman knocked on my

door and gave me two minutes to evacuate? I know people who have photo albums, hard drives, and jewelry in their go bags. Keep in mind that you may be evacuated to a center that can't provide for your needs, so always have some water, long-life food, and a change of underwear in case it takes a while for the situation to revert to normal.

A go bag needs to be able to be quickly accessed and light enough to carry easily. For this reason, I recommend a large daypack or duffel bag that has two shoulder straps. We've all seen the movies where the trained operative carries out their most important possessions in a duffel that they sling over a shoulder, and that's fine when you can move straight into a waiting vehicle, but if you have to walk for any distance, something that fits comfortably on your back is preferable.

I will now list my go bag contents, along with a quick explanation about each item. All these things fit into a snug 40L pack. Feel free to add or take out different items to your own personal preference, and use this as a guide rather than something set in stone.

GO BAG

WATER

- **All-weather lighter x 2**

  Can I make fire by rubbing two sticks together? Yes. Does this fire-making method burn up unnecessary time and calories? Yes. My idea of survival is making things as efficient and fast as possible, so I will most definitely include a few foolproof methods for fire making.

- **Water-carrying vessel**

  You can survive for about two to three days without water, but you will start to lose cognitive function before then. It's important if you are going to be processing water that you have something to process and carry it in. It is my preference that this vessel is stainless steel, so it can also be used as a pot to boil water if that becomes the only purification method available.

- **Ferro rods x 2**

  Lighters will eventually run out of fuel and have moving parts that can malfunction, so ferro rods are also a must, with the average rod offering between 8,000 and 12,000 sparks or possible fires and being impervious to weather conditions.

- **Water purification straws/tablets**

  These methods of purification will help make water drinkable on the go, or for times when making a fire to boil water may compromise your safety.

- **Emergency blankets x 2**

  Amazing for containing body heat, should temperatures plummet or water immersions occur.

- **Plastic ponchos x 2**

  Durable to keep dry during the wet, but can also double as a waterproof roof for a shelter; they usually fold down smaller than a waterproof jacket and can be used for other purposes, such as water containment and food gathering.

- **Small tarp**

  Great for shelter building, keeping in body warmth, general waterproofing, and also as a carrying tool.

- **Thermal tops and bottoms x 2**

  Always good to have warm layers for those colder times.

- **Socks x 2**

  Fresh socks can aid in keeping your feet in good condition; if your feet begin to deteriorate, then your chances of survival go down dramatically.

- **Underwear x 2**

  Not a necessity, but luxuries are always good for survival mental health.

- **Warm hat x 1**

  Contrary to popular belief, we don't lose a majority of our heat from our head, but we do lose about 7 to 10 percent, so it's worth having a hat for cold nights.

FOOD

- **Pot/cup/mess tin**

  Makes dinnertime a little easier; make sure it's stainless steel or similar, to allow for cooking and boiling water in if necessary.

- **Spork x 2**

  Building your own chopsticks is the best option for eating utensils in the outdoors, but sporks, which are a luxury item, don't weigh much or take up much room, and they make life a little easier.

- **Ration packs for three days**

  You can last twenty-one days without food, so this really is a luxury item; however, having access to something to fill your stomach until you can establish a food source can help with a good mental state of mind.

- **Paracord**

  The problem with cord is that it is a finite resource. For that reason, I tend not to use it for shelter building, as that requires a lot of cord for a single purpose. Where possible, I will use natural resources to hold my shelter together, but I will save paracord for such things as traps and snares; it is a wonderful resource for passive hunting techniques.

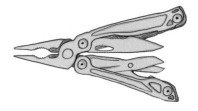

- **Fishing line and hooks**

  The line is useful for snares and traps, and durable hooks are incredibly tricky to make out of natural materials; they are reusable, and if you are by water, they are an incredibly efficient way of procuring food.

- **Multitool**

  A good multitool will have the versatility to aid you in a variety of situations. I personally find the saw blade and screwdriver heads to be the most useful. It can help you remain adaptable both in an urban environment and in the backcountry.

GENERAL

- **Field knife**

  If I am asked to choose only one survival item ever, then it will always be a knife. With the right ingenuity, skills, and problem-solving abilities, I can create everything I need with just a knife. This is possibly the most important item in this kit, so take your time in deciding on the right knife for you. I always have a minimum of a four-inch fixed-steel, full-tang blade that I have field-tested to make sure it works well for me.

- **Small first aid kit**

  I always travel with a stocked first aid kit, and my go bag is no exception; make sure it has any prescription medication that you can't live without. See page 283 for more information.

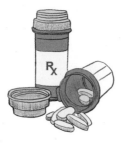

- **Headlamp**

  After having spent a lot of time in the outdoors at night without a source of light, I can tell you that not being able to see at night is a huge safety risk, and having accessible light can help immensely on a mental comfort level; it's best to have a headlamp with rechargeable batteries, but take spare batteries just in case.

- **Spare medicines**

  Best stored in the first aid kit.

- **Hand sanitizer/gloves/masks**

  For interaction with other people outside of your family unit, especially if your survival situation has come about during, or because of, a pandemic.

- **Spare batteries**

  In case the survival scenario becomes prolonged.

- **Dynamo radio/charger**

  This handy gadget allows you to crank a handle to create electricity to charge it and other items; it will also give you some access to news regarding your situation, if all other means of communication have failed.

- **Flashlight**

  Always good to have a backup light source.

- **Glow sticks**

  To be used for signaling for rescue, marking locations at night, or communication over distances.

- **Signal mirror**

  To be used to signal for rescue during the day; a flash from a mirror can be seen from up to a mile away.

- **Compass**

  Always valuable for wayfinding, if your survival situation requires you to travel any distances; a modern compass will also usually have a magnifying glass that will aid in fire making, should the weather be sunny.

- **Duct tape**

  I would use this more for repairs in an urban survival scenario, but no one can dispute the usefulness of duct tape; it is a finite resource, so use it sparingly.

- **Small solar charger**

  We all have a variety of devices that require charging to function; a solar charger allows for the longevity of these items.

- **Spare cash**

  If the survival scenario is urban and access to card transactions has failed, it's always good to have some cash on you to barter your way out of situations or buy supplies you need.

- **Photocopies of relevant documentation**

  Such paperwork as birth certificates, passports, and credit cards should be photocopied and carried in the go bag, in case the originals are lost and proof of identity needs to be established or money needs to be accessed.

As I said, these are my preferences from my experiences. Take your go bag out into the wilderness before a survival scenario strikes and see if you can sustain yourself for a short period of time with what you have chosen. Make notes, add and subtract items according to what you feel you would need, and get comfortable with your choices. A good go bag could save your life.

▶ FIRES

Fires can start suddenly and without warning. They can destroy homes, properties, and lives. One out of every one hundred people will experience a fire in their lifetime. The devastating effects of a fire decrease dramatically if you are prepared and act early.

Fire requires heat, fuel, and oxygen to stay burning. The more of these things a fire has access to, the more intense and damaging it will be.

Fires spread through three methods:

1. **Conduction:** where there is direct contact between materials.

2. **Convection:** when the air around the fire becomes hot enough to start new fires, if there is enough oxygen and a fuel source.

3. **Radiation:** when heat travels in rays similar to sunrays, in straight lines and away from the fire.

Smoke, heat, and toxic gases are all products of fire. Some are more obvious, but it can be the ones that are not so visible that take you by surprise and lead to your death. More people die from toxic fumes and smoke inhalation than from burns. During a fire, and in the aftermath, you may experience a variety of symptoms, including:

- Confusion
- Inability to breathe properly
- Disorientation
- Tiredness
- Fear
- Thirst

It is important to try to stay calm and take actions to ensure your survival. Having an action plan in place prior to the disaster will help you move through proactive steps, even if you are experiencing these symptoms.

Your initial response to a fire will depend on the time it has been burning and the ferocity of the flames. For instance, if your campfire jumps its boundary and catches nearby grass alight, you may be able to smother the fire with some dirt or put it out with your water bottle. If your house is in the path of a massive firestorm that is being pushed by gale-force winds, it is best to evacuate early, knowing that human lives are more important than staying to defend possessions.

What you do next will depend on where you are, the intensity of the fire, and your ability to get to safety quickly.

▶ WILDERNESS FIRES

Being out in the middle of nowhere when a forest fire starts can be terrifying. Chances are you will be surrounded by fuel and on foot, with very few options for your escape route. Trying to outrun a forest fire can be impossible; fire is able to travel up to 14 miles per hour in grasslands. If the fire is on an upward slope, it can double that speed, as the flames can reach more unburnt fuel faster. The heat radiating from the fire also preheats the fuel on a slope, which in turn causes the fuel to burn faster. A fire can also spread in any direction and change direction in seconds. A change in wind direction is one of the most dangerous factors in how a fire behaves. Many people who die in wildfires do so after a change in wind direction, so you will need to have a backup plan in case conditions change.

If you are present when the fire begins, or when it starts to get out of control, it is important to try to put it out if you can do so safely. Use any available water, or smother the fire to deprive it of oxygen. This can be done with such things as wool blankets, jackets, or dirt. If you don't have access to these things, try a branch of thick green leaves and beat the fire to squash it out. Just be careful that your efforts are not adding more oxygen to the situation by fanning the flames.

To ensure your campfire doesn't get out of control:

- Don't build a fire at sites with dry conditions.
- Build your fire away from your tent, trees, and bushes.
- Keep your fire small and manageable.
- Allow your fire to burn to ash before you leave.
- Pour water on the ashes until the hissing stops.
- Scatter dirt on the fire if you don't have water; make sure the coals remain exposed, and don't leave until they are cool to the touch.
- Don't cover your fire with dirt or sand, as this subdues it rather than smothering, it and the fire may catch back to life in windy conditions.

Once a fire is out of your ability to control it, you need to focus your energy on how to get to safety. Get safe, and then take a moment to make a plan. Your plan will be based on the following information:

- **The fire's access to fuel:** Are you surrounded by dry, dense forest, or are you in a wet, rocky area with very little vegetation?
- **Wind speed and direction:** Is the wind going toward you or away from you? The faster the wind, the faster the fire will travel; if the wind is strong, the flames can leap bigger fire breaks.
- **Your method of transport:** Are you on foot, or do you have a vehicle?
- **The terrain:** Where is the fire likely to spread to? Can you move quickly and easily to safety? Do you need to go uphill or downhill to safety?
- **Fire breaks:** Are there any natural fire breaks, including roadways, rivers, or lack of vegetation?

DO NOT RUN WILDLY. TAKE YOUR TIME, AND CHOOSE YOUR BEST ESCAPE ROUTE BASED ON ALL AVAILABLE INFORMATION.

If the fire doesn't start near you, some clues that a fire is approaching can be the smell of smoke, seeing smoke, or unusual animal behavior. Animals will flee ahead of a fire front and will be less cautious about human interaction. There will be a combination of animals that are not usually traveling together, and their movements can be agitated.

Do not think that because you can smell smoke but not see it that you have a lot of time to get out. Fire can reach you in under ten minutes from the time you smell the smoke.

To check which way the fire may be going if you can't see the flames, look high in the sky to see which direction the smoke is traveling. Wind can swirl in many directions on the ground, especially in mountainous terrain, but the smoke direction high up should be a good indicator of the way the fire is traveling.

If you are unable to outrun a forest fire, you can either find the best defensive position and hunker down or try to make it through the fire to the other side. These techniques are last-resort options. Always try to make your way to safety if possible.

▶ DEFENSIVE POSITION

Search your immediate area for a natural fire break. This can be a river, a road, or an area with very little to no vegetation. Clear the area of flammable materials the best you can with the time you have. Scoop out a trench in the ground on the opposite side to the fire, if you are able to. Cover all exposed skin with clothing, including your head and face. Dampen down the clothing, if you have water available. Drink to ensure you are hydrated. Lie in the trench with your feet facing the fire, and cover yourself with dirt. Try to stay calm and prepare your mind for what is to come. It may be loud, dark, and hot, but survivable. A deep gully might also work for a good defensive position. Lie low and flat against the rock wall closest to the fire; cover yourself with clothing and dirt the best you can. If the gully has dirt sides, try to dig a hole in the wall closest to the fire and crawl into it. Use a branch or stick to make digging easier.

Direction of fire

1.2.1.2

▶ OFFENSIVE POSITION

Run through the fire. If the fire is a slower, cooler fire, it may be possible to run through the fire to safety on the other, already-burnt side. This is not to be attempted for intense fires with a lot of fuel and high winds. It may be possible in a large clearing or with a low grass fire. Assess your position and your type of fire, and make a decision. If you decide to choose this option:

1. Cover as much skin as possible with material, and wet it down if you can.

2. Remove anything you are wearing that conducts heat, such as jewelry or a belt buckle.

3. Cover your nose and mouth with material.

4. Choose your spot carefully, aiming for an area where the flames are sparse and low.

5. Once you have made your decision and picked your route, don't delay.

6. Run as fast as you can until clear of the fire.

7. The ground on the burnt side may be hot enough to melt the soles of your shoes, so keep going until you reach a patch of cooler ground.

Create your own backburn. If the wind is blowing the fire toward you, and you have some time before it will reach you, consider creating your own backburn. This works well with grass fires and low-lying brush. Determine the wind direction and consistency, stand with your back to the wind, and light a wide line of fire in front of you. As this burns, it will deprive the following fire of its fuel and create a safe haven for you. Make sure that you have enough time for your fire to burn out a large enough area before the main fire reaches you, or else you will be trapped between two fires.

Being prepared for a fire in the wilderness means educating yourself about the terrain you are about to enter. Is it fire ban season? Has there been a drought in the area? Are you surrounded by flammable tinder waiting for a spark? Is the weather predicted to be hot and windy? If the answer to any of these questions is yes, then maybe consider changing your plans. If you choose to head out anyway, make sure you have appropriate clothing (natural fibers versus nylons, which are made of plastics that will melt and stick to your skin), bring plenty of water, and have an escape plan ready in case you need it.

Wind

1.2.2

▶ VEHICLES AND FIRES

Whether you get stuck in your vehicle during a fire, or your vehicle catches on fire, you need to be aware that you are traveling in something that could be either your best form of survival shelter, or a fueled bomb waiting to explode. Knowing when to leave the vehicle and when to stay could be the difference between a fire being deadly or an inconvenience.

1.2.2.1

▶ DRIVING THROUGH FIRE

If you try to escape a wildfire in your vehicle or come across a fire while driving, it is important to know what to do to ensure your best chance of survival. Try to drive out of the danger zone if possible, but if you can't:

1. Call 911, and let them know where you are and that you are in trouble.

2. Park the vehicle behind a solid structure, if available.

3. If no structure is available, find a clear area away from trees and bushes.

4. Park off the road with the front of the car facing the fire.

5. Turn off the engine.

6. Put on the headlights and hazard lights.

7. Stay inside the vehicle.

8. Shut the windows.

9. Close all air vents.

10. Get below the level of the windows.

11. Cover yourself with whatever you can find. Seat covers and car mats will work.

12. Drink water.

Stay down and inside the vehicle until the fire has passed. This may take between five and fifteen minutes. Once the fire has passed you, cover your mouth and nose with a cloth and carefully exit the car. Any metal will be hot, so take care when touching the car's surface.

Park off the road with the front of the car facing the fire.

Turn off the engine.

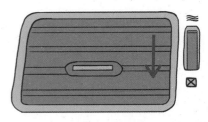

Put on the headlights and hazard lights.

Close all air vents.

Cover yourself with whatever you can find. Seat covers and car mats will work.

1.2.2.2

▶ VEHICLE ON FIRE

The first thing to do with a vehicle fire is to stop the car and turn off the engine. Get everyone out of the car quickly.

It is always important to have a fire extinguisher in your vehicle. Make sure it is inside the car rather than inside the trunk, in case the car has crashed and you cannot exit the vehicle quickly, or the trunk has been damaged and is unable to open.

If possible, it is important to control a vehicle fire to prevent it from reaching the fuel tank. If the fire is small and inside the vehicle, use a fire extinguisher to put it out, or try to smother it with whatever material you have at hand. Coats and bags will work well. Move away quickly after you have extinguished the flames, so you don't get overwhelmed by toxic fumes.

If the car has crashed and there is fuel leaking out, get out of the vehicle as soon as possible. If the fuel catches on fire, quickly move to a safe distance, at least one hundred feet or more from the vehicle. Call 911, and allow first responders to control the fire.

1.2.3

▶ FIRES OUTSIDE THE HOUSE

It is always good to have your house wildfire ready, regardless of where you live, but especially if you reside in a high-risk area. Your home is at risk if:

- The local area has a history of wildfires.

- You live near forests or bushland.

- There are many trees and bushes around your home.

- Your house is built on a slope.

- You need to travel through forest or grasslands to leave home.

- You reside where cities, towns, or suburbs meet grasslands.

- Your house is near coastal brush.

- You live close to grass or among paddocks.

A well-prepared house is more likely to survive a wildfire even if you aren't there. It can also be easier to defend and can offer more protection if fire threatens suddenly and you become trapped.

1.2.3.1

▶ PREPARATION AND PREVENTION

ESTABLISH A SURVIVAL PLAN

It is important to develop a plan of what to do if a wildfire threatens your home *before* one does. Talk this plan over with all the members of your household. Details will include:

- Meeting places, if you become separated

- Lines of communication

- When to evacuate

- Escape routes (always have a plan B)

- What to do with pets and animals

- What to take—have a go bag ready (see page 22) and a list of things to grab

Your list of last-minute things to grab should include:

- Driver's license
- Passport
- Photos/hard drives
- Will
- Jewelry
- Insurance papers
- Medical prescriptions
- USB containing important files
- Phone and phone charger

Some of these items can be stored together and ready with your go bag, if they are not needed on a day-to-day basis.

MAKE A FIRE EMERGENCY KIT

This is different from a go bag and need only be prepared if you are in a high-fire-danger area. Have the bag easily accessible and always ready. It should include:

1. Working battery-operated radio

2. Protective clothing: loose-fitting long pants and long-sleeve shirts made out of natural fibers, gloves, heavy-soled boots, protective eyewear, hat, and bandanna

3. Wool blankets

4. Water

PREPARE YOUR HOUSE

The time to prepare your house for wildfires is before the fire season hits. In most areas, fires rage in the hotter months of the year, so get organized in the cooler months before. Some things you can do to lower your chance of losing your house to a wildfire are to:

1. Clean out the gutters.

2. Repair any holes in the roof and/or replace missing shingles or tiles.

3. Enclose all areas under the house.

4. Clear surroundings of debris and undergrowth.

5. Maintain greenery by keeping it trimmed and to a minimum.

6. Know where your shovel and fire extinguisher are.

7. Ensure you have solid hoses that can reach all areas of the house.

8. Attach a fire sprinkler system to the gutters.

9. Establish a fire break if you live on a remote property.

10. Establish a water source that doesn't rely on electricity from the power grid.

Most people die in wildfires because they leave their home too late. By the time you smell smoke or see flames, the fire may be five to ten minutes away, and all your escape routes might be cut off. You can expect embers and spot fires moving ahead of an intense firestorm. There will be smoke, heat, and noise. You will be hampered by a lack of visibility and darkness, with fires approaching from any direction. Roads may be blocked by fallen trees, downed power lines, or emergency vehicles.

On extremely high-risk fire days, you should prepare as if a fire has already been announced:

- If the plan was to leave early, then evacuate.

- Keep an eye on local emergency service announcements.

- Move livestock to a safe area.

- Keep pets in a safe place and ready to be moved.

- Pack personal items and put them in the car.

- Face the car in the direction you will drive out.

- Remove anything from around the house that will burn easily.

- Turn off gas to the house.

- Block down pipes and partially fill gutters with water.

- Have your fire emergency bag ready.

- Close and lock all doors and windows.

- Unlock any side and rear gates to allow first responder access if needed.

1.2.3.2

▶ RESPONSE

Remember that the first thing you should do when a natural disaster strikes is to get out of harm's way. Listen to what authorities are saying; don't think you know best. If an evacuation order is in place, take your valuables and get out. Leaving early means getting away before there are signs of fire. Don't wait for a warning or siren. Don't wait to smell or see smoke. Enact your survival plan, and head for safer ground. If you can't leave your home safely, do the following:

1. Let someone know you are staying.

2. Get into protective clothing (see page 36).

3. Turn on the sprinklers.

4. Remove anything flammable from the outside of the house, e.g., outdoor furniture or doormats.

5. Shut doors and windows.

6. Tape across windows so they don't shatter everywhere if they break.

7. Keep an eye out for embers and put out spot fires. Burning twigs, leaves, and pieces of debris can float ahead of a fire, and sometimes precede it by hours, and they are the most common way homes catch fire in wildfires.

8. Decide on your best refuge in the house.

9. Locate a flashlight or headlamp.

10. Stay calm.

Out of the three ways a fire spreads, radiant heat is the main cause of people dying. This is because temperatures in front of a fire can soar to almost 3,000°F. The good news is that it only radiates in straight lines, so this lethal heat can be blocked by a solid object. Your best chance of survival if you are caught in a wildfire is to shelter in a solid brick building that has two points of exit. Your best refuge in your house will be a room that:

- **Is on the opposite side of the house to the approaching fire**
- **Is on the ground floor**
- **Has two exits, including one that leads directly outside in case the house begins to burn**
- **Has a clear field of vision toward the direction of the fire**
- **Allows you to stay away from windows**

Traditionally, people have filled the bathtub and sheltered in the bathroom. Bathrooms usually only have one exit, and it isn't to the outdoors. They also have frosted glass windows, so you can't keep an eye on the fire to know what is happening. Bathrooms also tend to be smaller rooms and more vulnerable to carbon monoxide poisoning, so they shouldn't be your first choice.

Once the fire front arrives at your house, seek shelter and actively defend the house from the inside by putting out embers and spot fires. Know that the fire will be very loud and very hot, and it will get dark. A single fire front normally passes within five to fifteen minutes.

Do not shelter in dams, swimming pools, or tanks. Radiant heat and smoke can still damage your face, head, and lungs. If you seek shelter in a large body of water, make sure you have something to float on or that supports your weight, as you may need to tread water for some time until it is safe to return to land.

1.2.3.3

▶ AFTERMATH

Survival is also about how you will recover in the days, weeks, and months after the fire. If you have evacuated, do not return home until authorities tell you it is safe to do so. Be careful of hazards on the road, including downed power lines, fallen branches, and escaped livestock. Look out for potential hazards when entering your home, as the fire may have compromised the structural integrity. Depending on the severity of the natural disaster, your survival scenario will be shaped by what you managed to bring with you in your go bag and the grace of others.

Above all, remember that things can be replaced but people cannot, so if you are standing in the wreckage of your place but you have all your loved ones with you, you made the right decisions.

1.2.4

▶ FIRES INSIDE THE HOUSE

Cooking fires are the leading cause of home fires, with electrical appliances and faults being the next. Cigarettes, heaters, and candles round out the top-five causes. Unlike wildfires, each of these methods of ignition requires a different method of extinguishing, and not knowing the difference could fan the flames rather than putting out the fire. House fires can happen in any house at any time, and there is no one location that is more prone to them than another.

1.2.4.1

▶ PREPARATION AND PREVENTION

Keeping an eye on any flame inside is a must, whether it is on the stove, by your bathtub, or on the end of your cigarette. In the United States, over 500 deaths per year would be prevented if more people made sure that their house wiring was up to code. You are twice as likely to die in a house fire if you don't have working smoke alarms, so make sure they are replaced every ten years and batteries are replaced whenever necessary. Always have a fire extinguisher in an accessible location, and know what type of fire the extinguisher is meant for. Most residential fire extinguishers are multipurpose and labeled ABC, but it is important to verify this before using it on different types of fires.

Types of fire extinguishers include:

- Class A—for ordinary combustibles, such as wood and paper

- Class B—for flammable liquids, such as grease, gasoline, and oil

- Class C—for electrical fires

- Class ABC—multipurpose

HOW TO USE AN EXTINGUISHER:

1. Pull or release the lock.

2. Aim at the base of the fire.

3. Squeeze or press the trigger.

4. Sweep it from side to side.

1.2.4.2

▶ RESPONSE

If you have caught the fire while it is small, attempt to extinguish it. This can be done by depriving the fire of oxygen, fuel, or heat. You can smother it with clothing, a heavy blanket, or sand. Only use water to try to put it out if it isn't caused by grease or electricity.

COOKING FIRES

These are usually only seriously ignited when caused by oil or grease. When your cooking oil becomes hotter than 375°F, it will start smoking and burst into flames. If you have a grease fire in the kitchen:

1. **Remove the source of heat by turning off the stove.**

2. **Remove the oxygen by covering the lit oil with a metal lid, if it is contained in a pot or pan.**

3. **Pour baking soda over smaller grease fires; this will smother the flames.**

4. **Use a Class ABC or Class B fire extinguisher to put out the fire.**

Do not use water on a cooking fire, as the water will sink to the bottom of the pan, become very hot, and explode, splattering burning oil into the air. Do not try to transfer the pot anywhere, since this may spill the burning oil onto the floor or more flammable surfaces.

ELECTRICAL FIRES

One-third of all home fires stem from an electrical fault. They tend to be difficult to identify, and therefore are more dangerous and destructive than other household fires. If your fire stems from an electrical fault:

1. Cut off the electricity—either at the plug or at the fuse box.

2. Remove the oxygen source by smothering it with clothing or a heavy blanket.

3. Use a Class ABC or Class C fire extinguisher to extinguish the flames.

Do not throw water on an electrical fire, as water is a natural conductor of electricity, and you may get shocked or electrocuted. Even if the electricity has been turned off, the appliance itself can store enough electricity to deliver a shock.

If the fire is too big to fight, it is important to evacuate immediately. If you have a go bag packed and accessible, grab it on the way out. Move away from the house, and call emergency services. Do not waste time collecting your valuables. No possession is worth dying for.

Smoke and toxic gas inhalation kill three times more people in house fires than burns do, so even if the flames are not threatening you, cover your nose and mouth with some material, get low to the ground, and head for the nearest exit. You may need to feel your way along the walls to find the door, if the smoke is thick. Feel the door with the back of your hand. If the door is hot or there is smoke billowing under the door, find another exit.

Trapped inside. If you cannot escape the building, go to a room as far from the fire as possible on the lower levels. Close all doors behind you and, wherever possible, put a solid object between you and the radiant heat. It may be tempting to flee upstairs away from the fire, but flames move faster upward than downward, so the lower you can get, the safer you'll be. If you can get to a room on the lower level that has windows but no doors, smash the windows to create an escape route. Use a heavy object rather than a body part to do this, as the glass will smash into jagged sections that can cause deadly bleeds. Make sure you remove the shards from the top of the window, and place some clothing or blankets over the lower ledge before crawling out.

If you have to escape through a room that is on fire:

- Remove any metal, including jewelry and your belt buckle.

- Cover all bare skin and your head with flame-retardant material, such as cotton or wool.

- Wet your clothing and coverings, if possible.

- Cover your nose and mouth with breathable material.

- Make a route plan, and avoid rooms with only one exit.

- Get down low.

- Don't hesitate once you have committed to going.

If your clothing catches on fire, exit the flames and immediately stop, drop, and roll. If you continue to run, this will fan the flames. If you are with someone who has caught on fire, encourage them to stop, drop, and roll, and try to help them smother the flames with extra clothing or blankets. Do not try to smother them with your body, as this may set you alight.

If you are trapped on the second floor, do not retreat into a room with no windows or doors to the outside. Get to a room that has the safest landing below its window or balcony. Look for a soft surface such as grass, try to avoid hard, uneven surfaces like rock gardens. Close the door behind you, and fill any gaps around the door with thick material, such as curtains or mats. Wet them if you can. Check the room to see if there is anything that you can tie together to make a rope—bed linen, curtains, and towels will all work. Use a reef knot (right over left, left over right) to tie them together, and test by putting some weight on the rope before you commit your full weight to it. If there is nothing in the room to make a rope out of, prepare yourself to drop from the windowsill or balcony.

People have died on the second floor of buildings believing they are too high up to get to the ground safely. The reality is that if you drop from a windowsill or a balcony on the second floor of a building, the average person is dropping less than six feet to the ground. A normal human body is able to survive the impact from a drop of up to thirty feet. Don't let your fear of heights lead to your death.

Throw any extra padding out of the room onto the ground below to add extra cushioning for your landing. Lower yourself out of the window backward, and hang from the windowsill facing toward the building. Push away from the building with one foot, and bend your knees on the landing. Use your arms to protect your head, and roll with the impact.

Only jump out face first if instructed to do so by emergency services with specialized equipment.

1.2.4.3

▶ AFTERMATH

Do not enter your home until instructed that it is safe to do so by first responders. Be aware that the fire may have compromised the structural integrity of your house.

1.2.5

▶ SKYSCRAPERS

If you work or live in a multistory building, take time to familiarize yourself with the escape routes. Take care to note the difference between an ordinary stairwell and a fire escape stairwell, and always prioritize using the fire escape. Avoid elevators in a fire, as they are designed to drop to the first floor and disengage once a building's fire alarm is activated. Do not hesitate once the fire alarm is raised. Your best chance of survival is to get out quickly, before the fire takes hold.

People who wait to take action when a fire starts are late to evacuate, have little to no protection, and end up sheltering in an unsafe environment. Know your fire danger, have a plan, prepare your home to best defend itself from flames, and prepare yourself for evacuation. Listen to authorities, and when in doubt, evacuate. No possession is worth losing your life or loved ones for.

▶ FLOODS

Floods are the deadliest type of severe weather. They occur where there is an overflow of a large amount of water beyond its normal limits, and usually dry land becomes covered or submerged in water. Floods can happen both in coastal areas and inland, and can be anywhere from a few inches deep to over twenty feet deep. There are so many casualties associated with flooding because it can happen rapidly, and the power of the water is usually underestimated. It takes only six inches of water to knock you off your feet, and a foot of rapidly flowing water is enough to move a car.

Floods are usually caused by one or more of the following:

- Heavy rainfall
- Overflowing rivers
- Broken dams
- Storm surge and tsunamis
- Lack of vegetation
- Melting snow and ice

The effects of floods can be devastating, with loss of lives, property destruction, and far-reaching economic impact. Even just a few inches of floodwater can do a lot of damage.

TYPES OF FLOODS

There are five different types of floods:

1. River floods: When the water rises above the level of the riverbanks: It usually happens because of excessive rainfall from tropical storm fronts, persistent thunderstorms, or combined rain and snowmelt; it can happen slowly or rapidly.

2. Coastal floods: When seawater encroaches on areas of land that usually stay dry: They are typically the result of a combination of tidal surges and strong winds caused by storms out at sea or tsunami events.

3. Storm surges: An abnormal rise in water levels in coastal areas usually caused by storms that create higher-than-normal tides due to a combination of high winds, big waves, and low atmospheric pressure, a storm surge is one of the more dangerous types of flooding, as it can happen very quickly and affect large areas at the same time; when a storm surge happens at the same time as a high tide, flooding as deep as twenty feet can occur.

4. Inland floods: Occur inland rather than on the coast. Usually caused by persistent rainfall over a few days or heavy rainfall over a short period of time, they can be catastrophic in urban areas, as there is nowhere for the water to go.

5. Flash floods: Can occur when there is intense rainfall over a short period of time They are the deadliest of all the floods, as they are extremely powerful and have enough force to move large boulders and cars, tear trees from the ground, and destroy buildings and bridges; these floods usually begin between three to six hours after rain.

It is important to know whether the area you live in, or are planning to travel to, has a history of flooding. Some terrain features that may be subject to flooding include:

- **River valleys**
- **Flood plains**
- **Low-lying coastal areas**

If you are spending time in these areas, it is best to make sure you are prepared for the possible chance of flooding.

1.3.1

▶ WILDERNESS FLOODS

Deaths caused by flooding on camping trips are usually the result of poor planning and a general lack of knowledge of what to do when these disasters strike.

Before heading into any wilderness area, check the weather forecast for the week prior. Floods are usually caused by heavy, persistent rainfall after long periods of dry weather. If your trip is taking you into areas with low-lying, river-filled valleys after such weather, it would be worth postponing the trip or heading elsewhere.

Study the map, looking not only at the route you have planned but also at the general terrain in the area and possible alternate routes out, should your initial plan become too dangerous.

Never make your camp in any of the following areas:

- **Next to the water's edge**
- **In dry creek beds or washes**
- **Below a high water mark**
- **At the bottom of a hill or ravine**
- **In a ditch**

Even if you can't see storm clouds and don't get a drop of rain at your camp, high rainfall in areas around you can funnel large amounts of water and debris your way quickly.

If possible, camp on spurs or at least 200 yards away from the edge of the water. If the water level starts rising, move to higher ground.

Flash floods may sound like a train or thunder coming toward you. If you hear this, immediately evacuate. You may have a matter of seconds to get to high ground before a wall of water and debris hits. Leave all belongings, and move as fast as you can.

If you get swept away in a flash flood, the important thing is not to panic. Turn onto your back and face your feet downstream. Keep your knees slightly bent to push off any objects or obstacles in front of you. Try to scull with your hands to move you toward the edge of the water, as this will not be moving as fast or as powerfully as the middle section. If you hit an obstacle, try to go over it rather than under it, as you may get trapped under the obstacle with a wall of water forcing you down. As soon as you can, make your way to the edge of the flood. If you have managed to get out of the floodwater by climbing a tree, stay in the tree as long as it is safe and wait for the floodwaters to recede. When it is safe, climb down and make your way to safety.

Shock and hypothermia may set in, depending on your location. Assess your basic needs to make sure that you can meet them. If you have lost all your gear, you may need to make your way out of the wilderness and to safety as soon as possible. Remember that all animals seek out higher ground when their land floods, so keep an eye out for panicked animals and predators out of their usual habitat.

Although you can never predict when flash flooding will occur, you can watch out for the weather signs that suggest it might happen. Never wait to evacuate. If you are unsure about the weather, err on the side of caution and move to higher, protected ground.

1.3.2

▶ URBAN FLOODS

The hard surfaces usually found in urban areas, such as roofs, roads, driveways, and sidewalks, make it harder for an excess of water to drain away. This means that less water is required to create flooding, and it may pool for longer than it would in rural areas.

1.3.2.1

▶ FLOODS ON THE ROADS

Never attempt to drive through floodwaters, if you are unsure of how deep they are. It is best to reverse away from the water and find another way to your destination. It only takes a foot of fast-flowing water to sweep away your car into deeper waters. Even if the water isn't moving rapidly, once water enters the tailpipe of a vehicle, it can flood the engine and cause the car to stall. Unless your car has a special snorkel for your exhaust, this means it will probably stall in a foot or so of standing water.

Do not drive across any bridges if they have water flooding over them. It is hard to tell how structurally sound the bridge is if you cannot see it.

As soon as your car stalls in floodwaters or begins to be swept away, you need to be making plans on how to exit the vehicle. **Do not call emergency services at this stage.** You may have a matter of seconds to act, and in this moment, you are the only one who can be proactive about your safety.

1. **Put down all windows and unlock doors. This needs to happen before your car goes underwater, as once water pressure builds up on the outside of windows and doors, they become impossible to open until the car is fully submerged.**

2. **Take off your seat belt; it is best to keep a blade or scissors in the glove box in case the belt has locked shut.**

3. **Exit the vehicle however you can; this may be through the door, window, or sunroof.**

If the vehicle is sinking, you will need to swim to safety. If the vehicle is remaining partially submerged, stay on the roof of the vehicle and wait for rescue. This would be the time to make the call to emergency services if you have your phone. If the water is less than knee-deep, you can try to walk to safety. Face upstream and shuffle sideways with your feet wide apart and your knees bent.

SUBMERGED VEHICLE If your vehicle has become submerged to the stage that you are unable to open any doors and windows, you will either need to break the glass or wait until the vehicle is fully submerged to open the doors. I suggest trying the former first, as it can be a very scary ordeal to wait for a car to fill up with water as it sinks. You will also need to be capable of relaxing and holding your breath for at least forty-five seconds as the final air leaves the interior of the vehicle and allows the outside to equalize with the inside.

The front windshield tends to be double-paned to withstand an impact, so your energy is best spent trying to break a side window. Use your foot, aiming for the upper edge, to see if you can smash the top of the glass away from its lower anchor points. If this doesn't work, remove the seat headrests and use the sharp underside to try to puncture the glass. A blade or

As soon as your car stalls in floodwaters or begins to be swept away, you need to be making plans on how to exit the vehicle.

Put down all windows and unlock doors. This needs to happen before your car goes underwater, as once water pressure builds up on the outside of windows and doors, they become impossible to open until the car is fully submerged.

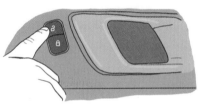

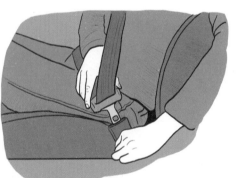

Take off your seat belt; it is best to keep a blade or scissors in the glove box in case the belt has locked shut.

Exit the vehicle however you can; this may be through the door, window, or sunroof.

scissors will also have sharp, solid points on them, which could be used to shatter glass. Aim at the top corners of the window. Keep your face averted to avoid getting shattered glass in your eyes. Car windows are made of tempered glass and will shatter in small squares that are less likely to cause deadly bleeds than large, jagged panes of glass. If you are unable to break the glass, take a moment to calm yourself. You will need to save your breath to wait to fully submerge.

One thing to be aware of is that a car can take two or three minutes to sink. As soon as you break the seal of the window or open the door, the car will sink more rapidly, so it is important that you exit the vehicle as soon as you have managed to secure an escape route. Do not wait for the vehicle to hit the bottom if it hasn't already. If multiple people are in the vehicle, make sure everyone is ready to leave before you open the door or smash the window. Once you have exited the submerged vehicle, swim for the surface and to safety.

Over 50 percent of flash flood deaths are caused by people trying to drive their vehicle through floodwaters. If you can't tell the depth of the water and/or if it is flowing rapidly across the road, do not attempt to cross. Not only does it put you and your loved ones in danger, but it also endangers those who may try to rescue you as well. Turn around and seek higher, safer ground.

The sharp underside of a seat headrest can be used to puncture the window.

▶ PREPARATION

If you are aware that the area you live in has a history of flooding, there are some things you can do to make sure that the damage to you and your property is minimal if history repeats itself:

- Make an evacuation plan; have two planned routes to high ground, designated meeting places if you get separated from those in your group, emergency contacts, etc.

- Sign up for flood notifications on your phone.

- Make a flood emergency go bag. Include such things as:

  - Phone charger
  - Flashlight and spare batteries
  - Blankets
  - Tarp/ponchos and/or emergency blanket
  - First aid kit

  - Rubber boots and gloves
  - Drinking water
  - Long-life food snacks
  - A signaling device (mirror or flares)
  - Radio to get accurate updates on flood

▶ RESPONSE

Always listen to the authorities. If they say to evacuate immediately, grab your go bag and leave the area for higher ground. If they say you have a few hours to prepare to evacuate, make your home flood ready and leave.

The aftermath of floods can be devastating to a home, but there are many things you can do to ensure that the damage is minimal.

1. Monitor the radio to keep an eye on the severity of the flood warning; you may need to stop what you are doing and leave at once.

2. Roll up any rugs and move furniture, electrical items, and valuables to higher ground; if your home doesn't have a second level, stack things on tables or benches—anything to get them off the ground.

3. Place important documents, USBs, and hard drives in waterproof cases; doubled-up resealable plastic bags work fine if you don't have anything else.

4. Empty fridges and freezers; take the food with you if you can.

5. Turn off the power, water, and gas.

6. Put sandbags in the toilet, and any drain holes in the bathrooms and laundry to prevent sewage from coming back up the pipes into your home.

7. Shut windows and doors, and seal up any areas that allow ventilation into your house.

8. Line sandbags along the bottoms of your doors.

9. Bring all outdoor furniture inside, along with any other items that may wash away.

If you are evacuating on foot, make sure that you do not cross any floodwaters that go above your knees. Find a stick or pole to use as a stabilizer and a depth probe. If the water is flowing rapidly, face toward where the water is coming from and walk sideways using the stick as a brace on the ground in front of you. Avoid drains and culverts, as a current can form near them that is strong enough to act like a vacuum that could suck you into them. If the water conditions are too deep and too strong or become that way, return to your home and establish a safe survival environment there.

If you are evacuating in a vehicle, do not attempt to cross floodwaters. If you are unable to find a route that doesn't require a water crossing, return home and establish a safe survival environment there.

SURVIVING A FLOODED BUILDING

If it is too risky to evacuate, stay where you are. Make sure that the gas and electricity are turned off. Shut all doors and windows, and sandbag the entrances. Grab your emergency flood go bag and some warm clothing, and move toward the upper levels of your building. This could be to the second story or the rooftop.

If you are seeking safety on the roof of your building, make sure that you are safely secured if the roof is steeply sloping. Use rope or sheets to tether yourself and others to strong, sturdy structures, such as chimneys. If you are able, establish some kind of shelter. Keeping in mind that clothing is your first line of shelter, this can be a poncho, or an emergency blanket wrapped around you.

Unless water rises so high that it forces you off this high ground, stay until the floodwaters have safely receded. Use your phone or emergency signaling devices to let people know you require assistance. Know that they may be dealing with more urgent cases than yours, so stay calm and get comfortable if your life isn't in immediate danger.

SWEPT AWAY If you find yourself swept up in floodwaters, do not panic. Turn onto your back, and face your feet in the direction you are going. Keep your knees slightly bent to help you push off any objects you might encounter in front of you, and try to scull with your hands to direct your body to safety.

Use rope or sheets to tether yourself and others to strong, sturdy structures, such as chimneys.

Unless water rises so high that it forces you off this high ground, stay until the floodwaters have safely receded.

▶ AFTERMATH

If you managed to evacuate before the flooding, do not return to your house until authorities have deemed it safe to do so. Be aware that the flood may have left your house structurally unsound, so be careful when entering the building and moving around until you have determined the severity of the damage.

Stay away from rooms where water still covers the electrical sockets, as water is a great conductor of electricity and may deliver a life-threatening shock.

Be aware that contaminated water may have penetrated the groundwater supply, and this will mean that your tap water is no longer safe to drink. Boil or purify all tap water until authorities have declared supplies safe to use again.

Do not eat food that has been in floodwaters, as the waters can be filled with bacteria, toxins, and chemicals that can make you very sick. You should also take care when cleaning up, making sure you wear rubber gloves and boots to minimize contact with any potential poisons.

Floodwaters can leave scenes of devastation, with debris, destruction, and corpses (animal and human). They are breeding grounds for stagnation, bacteria, and disease. Be prepared, listen to authorities, and evacuate sooner rather than later. It could be the difference between life and death.

1.4

▶ EARTHQUAKES

Earthquakes are the least predictable of the natural disasters, which makes them very hard to prepare for. They can come suddenly and with very little warning.

An earthquake is the sudden and violent shaking of the ground, caused by two blocks of earth slipping past one another at what becomes known as the epicenter. The sudden release of stored energy as this happens creates seismic waves that ripple through the earth's crust. They can be felt over large areas of land, decreasing in magnitude from the epicenter. Although earthquakes usually last less than a minute, their aftermath is devastating and has been responsible for thousands of deaths.

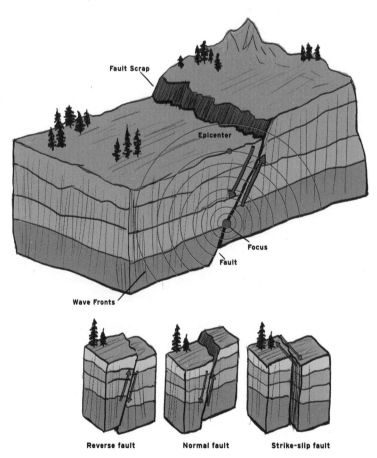

NATURAL DISASTERS

The effects of earthquakes can include:

- Ground shaking
- Surface faulting—when cracks appear in the ground
- Ground failure—sinkholes and unstable ground
- Tsunamis

The main causes of death are collapsing buildings and landslides, with over 3.5 million people worldwide being affected by earthquakes annually.

Earthquakes are fairly common, with over half a million earthquakes recorded globally each year. They range from subtle tremors to violent shaking, but only twenty will cause serious damage. Modern science still hasn't managed to find a way to predict earthquakes.

Earthquake severity is graded as follows:

2.5-5.4	May be felt slightly, but only causes minor damage
5.5-6.0	Slight damage to buildings and structures
6.1-6.9	May cause a lot of damage in populated areas
7.0-7.9	Can cause serious damage
8.0 >	Can destroy communities near its epicenter

The most powerful earthquake ever recorded was a 9.4-9.6 in Chile in 1960, but the deadliest earthquake on record was in China in 1556, with 830,000 casualties.

Minor tremors can happen anywhere, but major quakes are confined to known earthquake belts. There are over five hundred fault lines in California alone, and most people there live within thirty miles of one. It is important to find out if you live on one of these earthquake belts, in order to do what little preparation you can for these potentially catastrophic events.

1.4.1

▶ WILDERNESS EARTHQUAKES

If you are out in the wilderness when an earthquake happens, immediately move away from cliffsides and tall trees. Make your way to a clearing if you can, and lie flat; don't try to run. Cover your head with your arms. If you are on a hillside, it is safer to get to the top, as slopes may become landslides. Once the quake has stopped, make your way carefully to a place of safety.

1.4.2

▶ PREPARATION

The main thing you can do to prepare for an earthquake is to prepare for the aftermath. You can do this by having a go bag set up that will allow for you to last indefinitely without a functioning infrastructure (see page 22).

Some other things you can do are:

- **Identify solid safe zones in your house and place of work; these need to be areas that are structurally sound or will provide a solid roof over your head if the building (or part of it) collapses. Solid wooden tables or desks would work, as well as your bed. Down low against the inside corners of rooms and solid interior walls are also good options. Avoid any walls with windows or glass surfaces. Do not shelter under doorjambs. This advice worked when houses were built differently years ago, but doesn't work with today's building techniques and materials.**

- **Identify potential weaknesses and hazards in your home, so you know the areas to avoid.**

- Repair deep plaster cracks in ceilings and foundations.

- Attach large, heavy pieces of furniture to the foundation of your home.

- Use earthquake-proof putty to attach pictures and frames to the walls.

- Remove fragile items from high shelves, and place them in low cupboards.

- Ensure your shelves have lips on them, so things can't slide off.

- Make an emergency plan, so everyone in your household knows what to do and where to go if an earthquake happens.

1.4.3

▶ RESPONSE

Where you are when the earthquake strikes will determine your course of action, but the main idea, no matter where you are, is to:

1. **Stop: Do not try to keep moving, or you may fall and get injured.**

2. **Drop: Get close to the ground for more stability.**

3. **Cover: Seek cover under something solid, or cover your head if you can't find anywhere to get under.**

4. **Hold on: Grab on to something solid if the ground is buckling.**

As with any survival scenario, your ability to stay calm and think clearly will also help.

IN A VEHICLE

Once you are clear of underpasses and large trees, pull over and stop the car. Remain in your vehicle and try to get below window level. This will give you some protection if debris hits the roof of your car.

IN BED

If you are in bed, stay there. Turn onto your stomach, and cover your head with a pillow to protect yourself from projectiles and glass. If you have assessed your bed to be a safe place to take cover under, crawl under there as soon as the quake starts.

INSIDE A BUILDING

If you are inside a building, stay inside. A majority of deaths and injuries occur when someone is inside and they try to flee. If you are at home, head to your predetermined safe place. If you are at work, get beneath your desk or underneath something solid. Keep away from glass displays and shelving if you are in a shop. If you are in a high-rise building, stay where you are; never go into an elevator or try to escape down the stairwell until after the main tremor has ceased.

OUTSIDE A BUILDING

If you are outside, stay outside. Move away from anything that might fall on you, and if you can, relocate to an open area. Lie flat on the ground and cover your head. Keep away from tall buildings and large trees, and do not deliberately go underground or into a tunnel.

1.4.4

▶ AFTERMATH

As soon as the main tremors cease and debris stops moving around, check yourself and others for injuries. **If you live in coastal areas, make your way to high ground as soon as possible, as there is a chance a tsunami may follow.** Don't wait for authorities to advise you on this matter, because by the time you realize a tsunami is on its way, it's too late.

If you are in your home, check the water, gas, and power lines for damage. Stay out of affected areas of your house, and avoid or clean up any broken glass and debris. Turn on the radio to see what authorities are saying, and make sure you follow their instructions. Open cupboards carefully, and filter and boil all water until you have been told it is safe to drink.

If you are outside, do not enter or seek shelter in damaged buildings. Be aware of and avoid downed power lines and still-falling buildings.

TRAPPED

If you are trapped under large pieces of debris or have fallen down a sink-hole, cover your mouth and nose with some breathable material. See if you can move. If you are able to move, do so slowly to avoid causing further structural collapse, and try to make your way to safety. If you are unable to get out, try to find ways to make a lot of noise. Banging on exposed pipes, using a whistle, or smashing metal pieces together are all good ways of getting noticed by rescuers. Save your voice until you hear someone nearby.

The aftermath of an earthquake can stretch into days and weeks. The rupture of sewage systems, contamination of water, dead bodies trapped in wreckage, and disruption of infrastructure can be as deadly as the earthquake itself. Make sure that your go bag has enough resources to ensure your basic needs can be met indefinitely, and be aware that while you will be able to rebuild your life, you cannot replace it.

1.5

▶ HURRICANES

Depending on where you are in the world, the words "hurricane," "cyclone," and "typhoon" all describe the same phenomenon—an extremely deadly tropical storm with wind speeds in excess of seventy-four miles per hour.

They are called:

- **Hurricanes in the North Atlantic, central North Pacific, and eastern North Pacific**
- **Cyclones in the South Pacific and Indian Ocean**
- **Typhoons in the Northwest Pacific**

Hurricanes are destructive storms that are powered by strong winds circling around a center of low pressure, or the eye of the storm. They bring torrential rain and can occur at any time of year in any location, but usually occur in the Northern Hemisphere between June and November and in the Southern Hemisphere between November and April.

Hurricanes usually build up force out at sea and travel as fast as thirty miles per hour, wreaking devastation on islands and shorelines, and then slow down when they encounter land and the storm is cut off from the heat and moisture that fuels it.

There are different categories of hurricanes, based on the intensity of their wind speeds:

Category 1 (74-95 mph winds): Results in falling debris that may injure humans or animals. Older homes may be destroyed, and there might be short-term power outages.

Category 2 (96-110 mph winds): Extremely dangerous winds with greater risk of injury to humans and animals. Some houses may be damaged, and trees will be uprooted. There may be power outages that last anywhere from a few days to two weeks.

Category 3 (111-129 mph winds): Devastating damage will occur. There is a high risk that flying debris will result in injury and death. Well-built apartment buildings, individual houses, and industrial buildings will be damaged, and many trees will be uprooted.

Category 4 (130-156 mph winds): Catastrophic damage will occur, with a high risk of death and injury. All buildings will experience damage and power can be out for weeks or months. Infrastructure becomes severely damaged.

Category 5 (157 mph or higher): Massive destruction occurs. Only three such hurricanes have made landfall since 1924.

The problem with these categories is that they only take into consideration the wind speed of the event, not the expected rainfall or storm surge. This means that even a Category 1 hurricane can bring with it serious damage and risk, even more so because people underestimate its severity based on the category rating. Take all hurricane warnings seriously, and do the same for a Category 1 as you would for a Category 5.

Meteorologists can see hurricanes developing far out in the ocean, using satellite surveillance systems. This means that they can provide the public with a warning up to twenty-four hours prior to the storm making landfall. Hurricanes have been known to move erratically, though, so it is important to continue to listen for hourly updates once a warning has been issued.

▶ WILDERNESS HURRICANES

It is always important to check the weather forecast before you start a trip into the wilderness and to have some kind of method to check the updates if you are planning on being out for a long time. If you live in a place that is susceptible to hurricanes and you are heading out in hurricane season, carry a method to check weather updates no matter how long you are out for. Twenty-four hours' warning should be enough time for you to evacuate the area you are in and head for safety. Unless you can seek solid shelter where you are camping, you should never try to ride out a hurricane in the woods.

If you get caught unawares, you need to find the best place to shelter from strong winds, torrential rains, and possible lightning strikes. Stay away from the edges of water sources, as there may be flash flooding. Don't head for the highest ground, though, because this is where you are most exposed to the strong winds and lightning strikes. A deep cave would be ideal, as it allows you to move in far from the possibility of lightning strikes, out of the wind and rain. Do not shelter in overhangs or shallow caves, as lightning travels along vertical surfaces to seek the ground and can electrocute you as it jumps the gap.

If you can't find a cave, sit on the lee side (out of the wind) of any large object. Just make sure it is not the tallest object in your vicinity. If it is, you are better off lying facedown, flat on the ground with your hands covering your head. This will provide some protection from the debris flying around. Avoid small trees and fences, as they could be uprooted.

LIGHTNING

If your storm contains a lot of lightning, keep away from hilltops, ridgelines, tall trees, and lone boulders. Make for lower ground (being aware of the potential for flooding), and lie flat. If you cannot make it to low ground, find a dry insulating object and crouch on it with your head down, hugging your knees to your chest. **Do not sit or stand on anything wet.** If you have nothing to insulate you, lie as flat as you can.

If you see a flash of lightning and count before you hear the thunder, it will give you an idea of how far away the storm is. Simply count the seconds and divide by five to get the miles. Count "one hippopotamus, two hippopotamus," etc. to get the number of kilometers.

I have been very close to being struck by lightning while hiking on a ridge-line in the Blue Mountains in New South Wales, Australia. You can sometimes sense it coming when it is close by. My skin started tingling, and my hair stood up on end. I was also holding a fork that started tingling. These seconds of warning gave me enough time to drop the metal I was holding and hit the deck. The strike happened about thirty yards from me and was deafening, but I didn't receive a direct strike and was able to make it to cover for the remainder of the storm.

If you feel your skin tingle in a lightning storm, the best thing to do is to drop straight to your hands and knees. If you get struck, hopefully it will channel through your arms and into the ground rather than flowing through your torso and affecting your heart. As soon as you can, lie flat. Keep away from metal objects or structures. Proximity to large metal objects can be dangerous even without contact, because the shock waves caused by the heated air as lightning passes can cause damage to your lungs. An exception to this is your vehicle. If no buildings are available to shelter in but you have a car, this is the next best thing. Get inside, shut all the windows, and get down low, making sure you are not coming in contact with the metal exterior of the vehicle.

If you are on a boat, drop anchor and get as low as possible. If you can see a storm approaching, get out of the water as soon as you can. A significant lightning strike can stretch anywhere from six to ten miles from the base of the storm.

Education about the area and the weather conditions, plus a bit of preparation, could prevent loss of equipment, injury, or death. If possible, stay clear of wilderness areas until the threat of hurricanes has passed.

1.5.2

▶ PREPARATION

Even though meteorologists can give twenty-four-hour warnings prior to a hurricane making landfall, some preparations should be done well in advance. Tropical locations are more likely to be prone to hurricanes, and you can do some research to see the history of hurricanes in your area.

LONG-TERM PREPARATION

If you live in a place that may experience hurricane activity, you should:

- Make a household emergency evacuation plan; have multiple planned escape routes to high and sheltered ground if authorities issue an evacuation warning.

- Install storm shutters on your windows and glass doors.

- Buy a generator, and have about twenty-five gallons of fuel on hand.

- Trim trees and large shrubs around the home.

- Clean and clear all gutters and downpipes.

- Stockpile enough long-life food and water for seven days (one gallon of water per person per day).

- Install a bolted-down safe for important documents and valuables.

- Identify the best room to shelter in if you don't evacuate.

- Prepare a hurricane emergency bag (see sidebar).

- Prepare a go bag.

- Make a plan for your pets and livestock.

This should be the room you shelter in to ride out the storm. It should be an interior room, with no windows or glass doors and very little furniture on the lower level. A cellar is perfect. If your accommodation is not very structurally sound, make plans to go to the nearest hurricane shelter, or bunk with friends or relatives until the danger has passed.

Once the hurricane warning has been issued, the most important thing to do is to listen to the authorities. If they tell you to evacuate, then do your final preparations and get out. It is important that you leave far in advance of the hurricane making landfall, as travel in a hurricane is extremely dangerous and to be avoided. **Do not drive unless you must.** If you do need to drive, never attempt to drive through floodwaters, if you are unsure of how deep they are. It is best to reverse away from the water and find another way to your destination. It only takes a foot of fast-flowing water to sweep your car away into deeper waters. Even if the water isn't moving rapidly, once water enters the tailpipe of a vehicle, it can flood the engine and cause the car to stall.

If authorities are telling you to get ready but shelter on-site, do the final preparations and make your way to your safe room.

A hurricane emergency bag should contain the following:

- Battery-powered or hand-crank radio

- A NOAA weather radio with tone alert

- Flashlight

- Spare batteries

- First aid kit

- Whistle

- Charger and power pack for cell phone

Final preparations include:

- Stay informed, as hurricane updates could change at any moment; have the TV or a battery-operated radio tuned to the local news channel.

- Fill cars with gas, and move them to higher ground or put them in the garage if you are planning to stay.

- Charge all phones and devices; ensure power packs are fully charged.

- Bring all outdoor furniture inside, and secure any loose outdoor items.

- Place all important documents and valuables in the safe, or remove them from the premises.

- Fill all tubs and sinks with water in case water supplies become polluted or compromised.

- Unplug electrical appliances.

- Close all interior doors; this will help compartmentalize the pressure in the home into smaller areas, which reduces the overall force on the roof during a storm.

- If you don't have storm shutters on glass doors and windows, buy some ⅝-inch plywood from a hardware store and bolt it to the frames. Cover the whole window with a few inches of overlap on each side.

1.5.3

During the hurricane:

- Stay away from all windows, skylights, and glass doors.

- Don't walk outside to feel the strength of the wind, as even small debris can be dangerous.

- Don't use electronics that are plugged in, since there may be power surges.

- Do not watch the storm through the window, as flying debris and shattering glass could cause injury.

- Don't use running water if there is lightning, because if the house is struck, the pipes might conduct the electricity and travel it through the water.

- Stay inside until given the all clear from authorities. Hurricanes have a lull in them when the eye of the storm is passing over. It may feel like the storm is over, but it will start up again. Also, there may be hazards like downed power lines and fallen trees that need to be cleared before it is safe to venture out.

- Do not use your cell phone unless it is an emergency. Cell towers can get overwhelmed during natural disasters, and there may be someone trying to get through to emergency services with a life-or-death situation while you are calling your mom to say you are okay. Text your loved ones instead.

- Don't use charcoal or gas grills, generators, or propane stoves inside. This is because they release carbon monoxide that can quickly build up in unventilated spaces.

▶ AFTERMATH

If you have evacuated, return home only once you have been given the all clear from authorities. Avoid downed power lines and fallen trees as well as any other debris that may be hazardous to your vehicle.

If you have sheltered in place, administer any first aid required and cautiously move from your safe room when told it is okay by authorities. Assess the damage to your home, board up broken windows, clean up glass and hazards, and check for any damage done to your gas pipes. Find temporary accommodation if your home is unsafe. If major flooding has taken place, do not drink the tap water until it has been checked by a specialist. Filter and boil all water.

In severe weather events, you need to be prepared to lose electricity, fresh water, and sewage services for days and sometimes even weeks. You should have the right equipment in your go bag to be able to be self-sufficient until such time as repairs can be done and infrastructure reestablished. A majority of casualties occur when people do not want to prepare for the worst and then ignore warnings and evacuation orders. Expect the best, but prepare for anything.

▶ TORNADOES

A tornado is a tube of violently spinning air that touches the ground. It usually has the appearance of a funnel-shaped cloud and advances beneath a large storm system. Tornadoes can be among the most violent of storms, with a larger number of casualties than other storms, due to their unpredictable and extreme behavior, allowing for very little time to act. Falling and flying debris are responsible for the most deaths, as winds have been recorded at up to 350 miles per hour during a tornado.

Scientists are still not 100 percent sure what causes a tornado, but they surmise it is a change in wind direction and wind speed at high altitudes. This causes the wind to swirl horizontally. Rising air from the ground then pushes up on the swirling air and tips it over. The funnel of swirling air begins to suck up more warm air from the ground, and when the funnel touches the ground, it becomes a tornado. This mostly happens during strong thunderstorms called supercells.

Tornadoes can come in different sizes and shapes. Some may appear as wide, funnel-shaped clouds, and others like thin, rope-like swirls stretching from the ground to the sky. You cannot always see a tornado before it hits, and not all tornadoes will be visible. Some that are small or form in drier climates might not develop their funnels. These will look like swirling debris on the ground.

Tornadoes form in minutes and destroy large buildings, uproot trees, and send cars flying hundreds of yards. Most tornadoes last about ten minutes and travel approximately four miles, but there have been cases where tornadoes have lasted for several hours and traveled more than 150 miles. Their trail of destruction can be up to a mile wide. They can cross cities, mountains, and bodies of water and can occur anywhere in the world, but they are usually found in areas where warm, moist air meets cold, dry air.

Springtime usually brings the conditions that most commonly cause tornadoes, but they can happen at any time of year. Of the 1,400 tornadoes that occur on average worldwide every year, 1,000 of them occur in the United States.

Tornadoes are ranked according to wind speed on the Fujita Scale:

- **F0:** <73 mph wind speed, resulting in light damage

- **F1:** 73-112 mph wind speed, resulting in moderate damage

- **F2:** 113-157 mph wind speed, resulting in considerable damage

- **F3:** 158-206 mph wind speed, resulting in severe damage

- **F4:** 207-260 mph wind speed, resulting in devastating damage

- **F5:** 261-318 mph wind speed, resulting in catastrophic damage

Tornadoes are graded after they have passed through an area, based on the damage they have caused to human-built structures and vegetation.

Although tornadoes are hard to predict, these are some indicators that could suggest one is on the way:

- **Dark-, orange-, or green-colored sky**

- **Large, dark overhanging clouds**

- **Humidity**

- **Strong winds**

- **Large hail**

- **A loud roar**

If you encounter these conditions in an area that has a history of tornadoes, seek shelter immediately, regardless of whether an alarm has sounded or not.

▶ WILDERNESS TORNADOES

Facing a tornado out in the wilderness has the potential to be deadly. Escaping a tornado requires solid shelter or the ability to get out of the way. Tornadoes can move up to seventy miles per hour and have unlimited energy, so never attempt to outrun one. Use what time you have to find the best shelter option and hunker down. A cave would be the top option, but if you are unable to find one, seek low ground and try to create or find a ditch or depression to lie in. Place your arms over your head. Remember that most injuries happen from flying debris, so any way you can cover yourself will help.

If you have a vehicle, try to drive out of the way of the tornado, but if it is too late, buckle your seat belt and bend forward below the level of the windows. Cover yourself with a jacket or blanket, if available. Vehicle glass is made for impact, so it tends to be sturdier than house glass, but it will break with a direct hit from something heavy. Your seat belt will prevent you from being thrown around, should the strong winds move your vehicle.

Try to avoid going out in wilderness areas if storms are predicted, and always make sure you carry some form of communication device that will allow you to get weather updates if you plan on being out in the backcountry for a while.

1.6.2

▶ # PREPARATION

It is always a good idea to check the local natural disaster history in your area or an area that you're planning on visiting. If you are living in a region renowned for tornadoes, some important things to do before a tornado strikes are:

- **Make an emergency plan for your household. Include where to shelter outside the home, what to do when a tornado strikes, emergency numbers, and a safe meeting place once the tornado has passed.**

- **Get to know your local tornado emergency siren and what the alerts mean.**

- **Create a safe room or storm shelter. If you live in an area where tornadoes are common, creating an underground shelter is a good investment; this can be a purpose-built room outside of your house, or simply modifying the basement, if you have one.**

- **Identify where the local tornado shelters are in close proximity to your location. If you are caught outside your home when a warning is issued, it may be easier to make your way to your nearest shelter than trying to make it home.**

- **Create a tornado emergency bag:**

  - First aid kit
  - Flashlight
  - Spare batteries
  - Signal light
  - Battery-operated or hand-crank radio
  - Long-life food and water for three days

- **Create a go bag (see page 22).**

- **Make a plan for your pets and livestock.**

If you do not create a safe room, identify a room in your house that everyone knows will be the safe room. It would be ideal if this room is an interior room with no glass windows or doors. The less furniture in the room, the better. Bathrooms work well as the safe room for tornadoes, as they are usually fortified by pipes, and you can lie in the bathtub and cover yourself with a mattress, pillows, or blankets.

1.6.3

▶ RESPONSE

Tornadoes are extremely hard to predict. If an evacuation order is issued, you may only have minutes to get out. Always have your go bag ready and in an accessible place, and leave everything else behind.

Tornado alerts are issued as follows:

- **TORNADO WATCH:** Watch and prepare for severe weather.

- **TORNADO WARNING:** Get to shelter now; you may have only minutes.

- **TORNADO EMERGENCY:** There is a tornado confirmed in the area.

When a tornado watch is issued:

- **Secure all outdoor furniture and moveable objects.**

- **Close all doors and windows:** The myth that opening some or all windows helps in a tornado has been disproven, and it is recommended that you keep them closed; open windows can create a pressure vacuum that may result in strong winds lifting your house off its foundations, and it also lets in debris that can cause more damage.

- **Close blinds and curtains.**

- **Turn off all utilities.**

- **Park vehicles in the garage, if possible.**

- **Grab your emergency bag and go bag, and make your way to your safe room.**

- **If you are on the road, drive to your nearest shelter if you are not close to home.**

- **If you live in a mobile home, it is best to make your way to the nearest storm shelter.**

When a tornado warning is issued, you should already be in your safe room. Get down low, and cover yourself with a blanket. Stay calm and positive for those around you. Keep the radio tuned to your local news station, and do not leave the room until authorities have declared it safe to do so.

If you are not home when a tornado warning is issued:

- Take shelter in the most solid structure available.

- Go to the smallest central room on the lowest floor of the structure (staying out of elevators).

- Keep away from windows and glass doors.

- Do not go outside.

- Do not try to outdrive a tornado in an urban area; seek shelter instead.

- Do not shelter under overpasses or bridges in your vehicle; the wind can become more intense under these structures and funnel in debris.

If driving has become dangerous, pull over away from any trees or structures, stay in your vehicle, keep your seat belt on, and lean forward to try to get your head beneath window height; cover yourself with a coat or blanket, if you have one.

Although it is frequently said that you can hear a tornado coming, the wind often only picks up before the tornado arrives, so do not wait until you hear it to act, as that may already be too late.

1.6.4

▶ AFTERMATH

Always wait until given the all clear by authorities to leave your shelter or return to your house if you have evacuated. Be aware of any hazards that may have been caused by the strong winds, such as downed power lines and uprooted trees.

When leaving your safe room or returning to your house, take care to avoid any broken glass or structural damage. If your house is no longer structurally sound, seek shelter elsewhere. Check all utilities to see if there is any damage to gas or power lines. Do not use an open flame if you suspect there may be damage to gas lines.

Be aware that you may be without power for a few days or weeks, depending on the severity of the tornado. Ensure that your go bag has everything you require to meet your basic needs over this period.

Tornadoes can be very scary to contemplate if you have never experienced one before, but for many people in certain parts of the United States, they are simply part of life. Being proactive before one hits, and staying calm during, can increase your chances of making it out alive.

▶ TSUNAMI

A tsunami is the deadliest of all ocean disasters, with the potential to level entire cities. Tsunamis can travel up to five hundred miles per hour and reach heights of over one hundred feet before piling up against the coastline. They can strike without warning, and there is little that can be done to prepare and defend against a moving wall of water. Tsunamis produce unusually strong currents, rapidly flood land, and devastate communities.

A tsunami is a series of ocean waves, usually caused by one of three things:

1. **Earthquakes**

2. **Landslides**

3. **Volcanic eruptions**

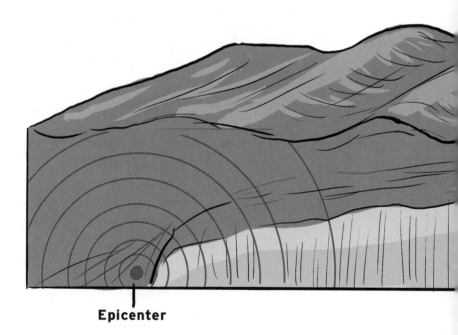

Epicenter

The wave will start at the epicenter and radiate outward in all directions. The first wave to hit the shore is usually not the strongest. The successive waves will get bigger and stronger. A tsunami can be up to a hundred miles in length, and the waves can continue for days, resulting in loss of life, mass injuries, and damage and destruction of homes, infrastructure, and facilities.

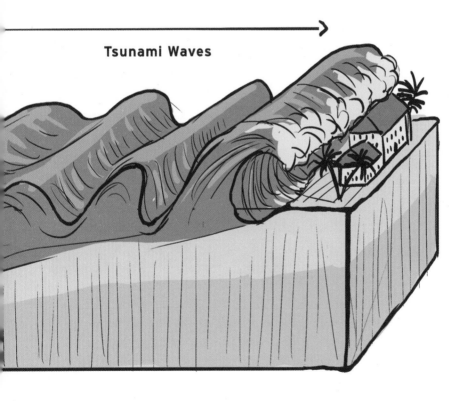

Tsunami Waves

There are two types of tsunamis:

1. Local: These are large waves that have a source close to shore and can arrive in less than an hour; they are more dangerous, as there is less time to evacuate and get to safety.

2. Distant: These are large waves that have a source farther out to sea; they are less dangerous, as authorities have more time to issue warnings, and people have more time to respond and get to safety.

Most damage in a tsunami is caused by:

- **Flooding**
- **Wave impact**
- **Strong currents**
- **Erosion**
- **Debris**

Although tsunamis can happen anywhere, there are well-known, high-risk areas along the coasts in the Pacific Ocean. On average, there are two tsunamis per year that are destructive, and about 80 percent of all tsunamis happen in the "Ring of Fire," a chain of active volcanoes that runs for almost 25,000 miles (40,000 kilometers) around the Pacific Ocean.

Be aware if you are choosing to travel to or live in an area that has been impacted by a tsunami in the past. Areas to have a good emergency plan if you are spending time in them include:

- Beaches
- Bays
- Lagoons
- Harbors
- River mouths
- Low-lying coastal areas

Scientists have developed early warning systems that can accurately predict when a tsunami can make landfall, based on the depth of water, the distance from one place to another, and the time the trigger occurred. However, this does rely on them having sensors in the right place on the ocean floor when the trigger goes off, so it is important for you to know what to look for in nature that may indicate a tsunami is on its way.

Some of the indicators in nature include:

- A significant earthquake felt along the coast
- Rapid rise and fall of water on the shorelines
- Pets and animals acting strangely

After noticing these signs, you may have less than twenty minutes to get to high ground, so move swiftly.

1.7.1

▶ PREPARATION

Surviving a tsunami is going to be all about how quickly you can mobilize and retreat to higher ground. This means that you will need to have your best evacuation routes from home, school, and work memorized, along with a backup if traffic is jammed.

A safe place will be at 150 feet above sea level or two miles inland. Plan both vehicle routes and ones you can travel on foot. If you don't have a plan, simply head uphill however you can.

It's also a good idea to:

- Have an emergency plan for your whole household, and make sure everyone is familiar with it; know where your safe area is, map out routes from home, school, and work, and aim to meet during or after the event if you are separated.

- Educate yourself about tsunami warnings in your area, official and natural.

- Have a go bag packed and easily accessible (see page 22).

- Have a plan for pets and livestock.

1.7.2

▶ RESPONSE

If your tsunami is preceded by an earthquake, follow earthquake protocol (see page 70) until tremors cease, and then follow tsunami protocol.

It is always better to be safe than sorry, so don't take any chances in tsunami areas if any of the warning signs occur. Get out, and get out quickly. Head to higher ground by whatever means you can as fast as you can. Stay out of the water, away from beaches, and avoid waterways.

Most buildings are not designed to withstand the impact of a tsunami; however, the upper stories of some buildings may be able to provide protection if no other options are available.

The levels of authority warning are:

Tsunami watch: This is when a tsunami may later impact the area; begin to gather your family members and valuables together, and have radio updates going all the time in case the status changes.

Tsunami advisory: This is when a tsunami with the potential to generate widespread damage is imminent, expected, or coming; evacuate low-lying coastal areas immediately.

Tsunami warning: Take the same actions as with an advisory.

If you get caught in a tsunami, do not try to swim. Grab hold of any passing floating object, and let the current carry you. Turn so that your feet are facing downcurrent, and keep your knees slightly bent to allow you to push off any objects that you encounter under the water. Try to go over objects you come up against rather than under them. If you see any high ground or a place of refuge, use your hands to scull toward it. Be aware of debris in the water with you.

Once the forward energy is spent, the water may retreat back into the ocean if it has nowhere else to go. This will produce an outgoing wave that can be as dangerous as the ingoing one, so make sure you try to find a secure position before this occurs and hold tight.

If you are in a boat during a tsunami warning, head out to sea. The deeper the ocean, the lesser the wave.

1.7.3

▶ AFTERMATH

Do not return to low ground until authorities have given you the all clear. Tsunami waves can last as long as a few days and have hours between them.

Depending on the severity of the tsunami, your home may range from having no impact, to flooding, to complete destruction. Take care to avoid hazards such as downed power lines and uprooted trees as you make your way home. In the event of a major tsunami, be prepared for infrastructure to be compromised and the possibility of a survival scenario that may stretch into weeks.

▶ EMERGENCY PLANNING

What you choose to include in your emergency plan can be as varied as what you decide to put in your go bag. However, a good emergency plan for all natural disasters should include:

Hazard identification and assessment: What is your most likely natural disaster, and how serious could it be?

What can you do to prepare or prevent the disaster?

Emergency resources: What infrastructure is in place in your local community to help combat the disaster?

Communication systems: Have all relevant phone numbers stored, emergency contacts established, and an alternate means of communication, should phones be lost or batteries die.

Emergency response procedure: What are the steps you will follow if you are evacuating, or if you are staying in place? Have at least two evacuation routes established and rehearsed, and two meeting places established if the household gets separated. Have routes planned from your workplace, home, and school.

Communication of the procedure: It is important that the whole family knows the plan. Awareness of a threat shouldn't lead to fear of a threat. Being prepared and letting everyone know how prepared you are can ease the fear of the unknown.

Create a go bag: Make sure it can cover all your basic needs for the whole family for at least three days or more (see page 22).

▶ AFTER THE DISASTER

A natural disaster doesn't end when the event burns itself out or loses momentum. For most people, this is when the true survival scenario begins. You and your loved ones may be safe from harm, but what if you return to a site of devastation and destruction? And you are not alone? The emergency services may be overwhelmed as your neighbors and community, and perhaps even the state or country, battle to come to terms with what has happened. The demand on emergency resources will be high, and people can react with fear, shock, and anger to such an event. This is when you will need to stay calm and make proactive decisions, relying on your good preparation and knowledge of your basic needs to get you through. You are now in an urban survival scenario, and you need to know how to manage it for the immediate future, and what your priorities will be if it takes weeks or months to rebuild.

2

Urban
Survival

URBAN SURVIVAL IS A COMPLETELY DIFFERENT scenario from surviving in the wilderness. You may have access to more resources, but you will likely be competing with scared, desperate, and hungry individuals and groups of people that may become violent and threatening when they feel like their life is on the line. Limited supplies quickly turn friendly faces in the streets against one another, and anything accessible is considered fair game.

You may need to use your urban survival skills in the days and weeks following a natural disaster, in a pandemic, and in times of war and civil unrest. These skills will also be helpful if the power grid goes down for a few days in extreme heat or storms have downed power lines in your region, leaving you without utilities for weeks. It doesn't take long for your home to become an icebox in a blizzard without access to heating, and the exposure rules of three hours of extreme cold before death apply in cities as well as out in the woods.

If you survive through a natural disaster, you may be lucky enough to find that your house is still standing with minimal damage and all utilities are still functioning. You may also return after an evacuation to devastation, but have a place to retreat to while you rebuild your home and life. The situation gets dire if you return to your house to find it damaged or destroyed, but you have nowhere else to go. This may be because it is a widespread catastrophe, and infrastructure is not functioning for days leading into weeks. The people around you have been impacted as well, and the demand for emergency relief far outweighs the help available.

Power will be one of the first things to go that will make communication and staying informed difficult. Society is so dependent on technology to help with these things that it is almost incomprehensible to consider that there may not be access to devices once batteries are dead. Always have a charger pack in your go bag as well as another method of renewable energy, such as a small solar panel. If you live in an area that has a history of losing power during natural weather events, it is worth investing in a generator and keeping thirty gallons of fuel in storage for it. This should last at least five days if you are running it for eight hours a day, so use it sparingly if it looks like you may need it for longer than that.

Your go bag should also contain a battery-operated or rechargeable radio. This will help you stay informed by listening to local news channels.

You will need to make your home your own personal life raft and work to ensure the survival of all those who are a part of your team. It will be time to get creative. One person's trash is another person's treasure; be adaptable, and stay positive for those who are struggling with the dire change of living conditions.

2.1

▶ GETTING HOME

Your emergency plan will have covered where your household should meet when disaster strikes. Hopefully you all made it out together, but if you didn't, call each other, call emergency contacts, and check all meetup locations to band together. Wait until authorities declare it safe to return to your area before traveling back to your house. Be aware of hazards from the disaster, making sure to avoid flooded areas, downed power lines, and fallen trees.

Your car should be equipped with a car emergency kit, as well as having your go bag, in case you are required to spend a few days away from home before returning. These kits will ensure that you can take care of yourself and your loved ones in whatever emergency shelter situation you end up in.

2.2

▶ SHELTER

Once you have made it back to your house, assess the damage from the outside first. How badly is your home affected? If the disaster has left your residence structurally damaged to the point of collapse, do not try to shelter inside.

This being the worst-case scenario, salvage materials from your house and yard to build a shelter outside of your house. Sheets of plywood, beams, bricks, and furniture will all contribute to building a sturdy shelter for you and your family. Depending on your disaster, you may need to cover your shelter with a tarp to stop the rain from getting in or use a table to get off the ground. Build the shelter at the back of the house if possible, as it will be easier to fortify and will also shield you from opportunistic looters.

If your house has some damage but is structurally sound, choose the best room for everyone to bunk in and make that your base. Keeping everyone together will be safer but also use fewer resources to warm if heating is an issue. In extreme cold, choose the smallest room in the house, and cover windows and doors with sheets and blankets to prevent the heat from escaping. Place mattresses together, and cover them with as many blankets and duvets as you can find.

Assuming access to electricity, water, and gas has been cut off, you will need to begin to make provisions for basic sanitation, as toilets will not flush in these scenarios. If you have access to a large water supply, such as a swimming pool or rainwater tank, you may keep using your toilet, but you will have to throw a bucket of water down into the bowl after use. In order to save water, only "flush" when you need to, rather than every time you urinate, and only use minimal toilet paper.

If you have limited access to water, you will need to find an alternative. One option would be digging a hole in your backyard. It would be best if it was one deep hole and filled in as people use it, rather than multiple holes each time you need the bathroom. Another option is a bucket lined with a plastic bag. Some suggest lining the top with a pool noodle for comfort and using kitty litter to sprinkle on as you go. The only problem with this method is disposing of it once you are done, as garbage collection usually vanishes if a town's infrastructure does. It is, however, the best method for apartment buildings or places without a backyard.

Disease becomes rife in these kinds of scenarios, so make sure you use hand sanitizer after each toilet visit, especially if you don't have access to water to wash your hands.

2.3

▶ WATER

If you are located in an area that has a history of natural disasters, you should have at least three days' worth of water stored somewhere in your house for such an emergency.

Natural disasters have the potential to contaminate the groundwater that is fed into your plumbing. This means that until local authorities have declared it safe to consume municipal water, you shouldn't use it for drinking, cooking, washing your hands, or bathing without purifying it first. If your electricity is off, chances are your water supply will be too. Unless your house is gravity fed, water requires electricity to pump into your house and out your taps.

Water that has been contaminated by toxic chemicals or fuel cannot be made safe to drink by adding disinfectants or by boiling, so if you suspect that this is the case, find water from elsewhere.

It is a good idea to familiarize yourself with your closest bodies of water prior to an emergency. These could be lakes, rivers, dams, or a local swimming pool. All water will need to be purified before drinking, and if there are chunks, I suggest filtering it as well. If you are using it for toilet water, you can use it as you find it.

In a shorter-term urban survival scenario, it is good to ration half a gallon per person per day for drinking water and half a gallon for cooking, washing, and sanitation. Some places to access water around the home will be:

- **The toilet tank:** Don't use water from the bowl, as that water will be polluted by bacteria. But the tank that supplies the bowl will hold about four gallons on average, and that can keep a family of four going for a day; make sure that there are no deodorizers or chemicals in the tank before purifying and consuming.

- **Hot water heater:** The average water heater will hold anywhere from six to a hundred gallons of water. Just be careful that the water isn't scalding hot when you access it.

- **The bathtub:** If you managed to fill it before the power went out, the average bathtub can hold forty-two gallons of water.

- **Water tanks:** You may have a method of catching and storing rainwater, which will ensure a good supply of water.

- **Swimming pools:** This water is good for flushing the toilet and washing clothing but will need to be purified and distilled to make it drinkable, depending on how maintained it is and the method of treatment used to keep it clean. If the chlorine levels are less than four parts per million, the water will be safe to drink after bringing it to a boil. Anything more than that will need to be filtered using a purpose-built water filter, then distilled using evaporation to separate the pure water from the chemical impurities. There are many different and complex ways to distill water. The basic idea is that you need to heat the water so that the pure water rises from it as steam. This steam then needs to be collected and cooled in such a way that it reverts to liquid form, this time without the impurities in it. If you have some pipes and collection pots and perhaps some duct tape, you could rig up an efficient system to keep many people satisfied with drinking water indefinitely.

A simple water still could be put together by collecting the pool water in a pot and devising a cover for the pot that has a pipe rising from it and traveling to another container. Place the pot over a heat source. When the water begins to steam, the system should allow the steam to rise from the pot and travel through the pipe, where it cools back to liquid form and runs downward into the collecting container. This water will be good to drink.

Toilet tank

Bathtub

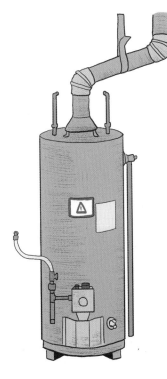

Hot water heater

Swimming pool

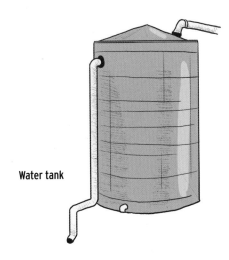

Water tank

Some other simple water stills are mentioned below.

RAIN If your disaster is accompanied by rainy weather, it is a good idea to try to catch and store as much of the rain as possible. This can be done by redirecting gutter downpipes and/or creating catchment areas with buckets or any other containers you can find.

PURIFYING

The best way to ensure that the water you drink is safe is by boiling it. This requires using electricity, wood fire, or fuel for your stove in your go bag. If the electricity is off, wood and fuel may be limited in an urban survival scenario. Your go bag should be equipped with at least two other methods of purifying water, including a water filter and/or purification tablets. If you don't have access to either of these, you can create your own urban distillation process.

WATER STILL

There are a couple of ways to do this, but they both require direct sunlight or heat, so if you are experiencing cloudy weather or want to save fuel, choose another method to purify your water.

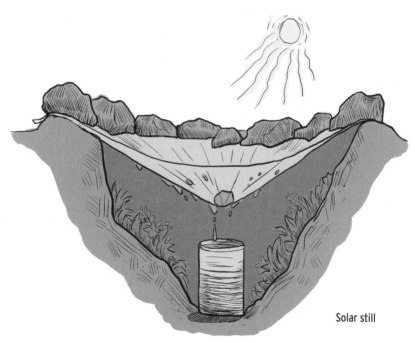

Solar still

Fill a tub with the water to be distilled; this still works on the same principle as a wilderness solar still. Place an empty container in the center of the tub; weigh it down so it doesn't float. The water in the tub should not be high enough to flow into the empty container. Cover the tub with clear plastic, and place a rock in the center of the plastic so it dips down where the empty container is, without touching it. The water will evaporate and recondense on the surface of the plastic, where it will drip into the empty container. This water will be drinkable. If the tub is metal, or you have a larger metal container to use, you can apply heat to the bottom of the tub to speed up the process.

Another method requires a clear water bottle and a can. Cut the bottom off the water bottle and the top off the can. Fold the bottom sides of the water bottle up into itself to create a gutter to catch the distilled water. Fill the can with pool water, and place it inside the water bottle. Make sure the lid is on the water bottle, and place the still in the full sun. The water will evaporate from the can in the heat and re-form on the inside of the water bottle, sliding down the sides to be caught in the gutter. This method takes time and sunny weather, so make multiple setups, if possible.

CHEMICAL PURIFICATION

If you do not have specific water purification tablets, you are able to safely use bleach as an alternative. Add eight drops to a gallon of water and wait thirty minutes, and then it will be safe to drink.

Iodine also works, if there is any in your first aid kit. Add thirty drops to a gallon of water, and wait thirty minutes before drinking. Iodine aggravates thyroid conditions, so avoid this method if you have any issues.

Do not drink radiator water under any circumstances. Quite often this water is mixed with coolants or antifreeze, both of which are toxic to humans.

2.4

▶ FOOD

Your go bag should be stocked with three days' worth of emergency rations. This is the average time that it takes for services to resume after a disaster. Take stock of what long-life food you have in the house, and create a meal plan that will enable you to make it last for as long as possible.

If electricity is compromised, your refrigerator and freezer will not work. Eat the food that will spoil first. Do not eat refrigerated perishables after one day in hot climates and two days in cooler climates.

You can extend the time that your fridge stays cool by not opening the door very often or for long periods of time. This will keep the colder air in for longer. You can also put food from the freezer into the fridge. The frozen goods will act like ice blocks and allow you to get an extra day out of your perishable foods.

This is one of the areas that survival is easier in the outdoors as the days stretch into weeks. It is much easier to forage for wild edibles in most wilderness areas. There are some common weeds that grow in urban environments that are great edible weeds, but make sure that you harvest them from areas that you know haven't been subjected to weed killer or other toxic chemicals. It is a good idea to wash them thoroughly before consuming, due to human and animal pollutants as well.

Some plants you may find in urban areas are:

MUSTARD A common plant found all over the side of the road, its edible yellow flowers have quite a spicy kick, and the young leaves are good for a salad. The mustard plant belongs to the same family as vegetables like cabbage and broccoli. As such, it has many of the same nutrients; it is very high in vitamins A and C and serves as an antioxidant.

SUNFLOWERS The raw seeds of sunflowers are very high in protein, and the flower buds (before they bloom) can be cooked and eaten like artichokes. The hulls of the seeds are a good source of fiber but need to be ground up to avoid sharp pieces damaging your mouth and throat.

DANDELIONS High in calcium, magnesium, and iron, dandelions are also used medicinally and are helpful if you are having digestive trouble. The green leaves can be eaten raw in salads or sandwiches and have a tangy, slightly bitter taste. You can also boil them briefly to remove some of the bitterness. The root, stripped of its outer fibrous layer, can be eaten raw if taken from young plants, or dried and ground to make a good substitute for coffee.

THISTLES These are among the hardest wild plants to gather, on account of their spines, but they are edible. The stalk can be peeled to rid it of its spines, and then boiled before eating. The roots can be dug up and eaten raw or cooked, while the leaves should be stripped of their spiny green parts to leave the edible "rib" down the middle. Eat raw or cooked.

STINGING NETTLES Wear gloves to make sure you aren't stung collecting the leaves, but once nettle leaves are boiled, the irritant is gone and they taste a lot like spinach.

Remember, there are far more edible plants in the world than there are poisonous ones, but you only need to make one mistake and it can be fatal. Make sure you know you have the right plant before eating.

In urban survival scenarios, it is better for you to remain in your home if possible, as society can descend into a chaos of lawlessness and looting. Do not go out until your life depends on it.

If weeks stretch into months and there is no end in sight, you may need to head into your local wilderness areas to hunt for bigger game. My local park is filled with rabbits and is a five-minute walk away. The local bird life would also become a good, targeted food source. Be vigilant with your weapon safety, and ensure you have a safe backstop before firing a weapon in an urban area.

Assume that most food stores will have been stripped of all available consumables by the time you need to start seeking food if your disaster preparation was solid, but it is a good idea to scavenge what you can from your immediate area. This isn't looting; it is survival. If your neighbors haven't returned and a month has gone by, raiding their cupboards for your family's survival is forgivable.

2.5

 # FIRE

In an urban environment, you should be able to find enough warm materials to see you through the night without a fire, if the temperatures don't drop way below zero. Unless you live by a wilderness area or have a wood-fueled fireplace with a stock of winter fuel, wood will be a limited resource. You may need to make a fire to cook on or purify water. If this is the case, keep it small and contained.

Methods of lighting fire should be easy to come by, although they may be finite materials such as matches and lighters. Make sure you do not waste them even if it seems that you have plenty, because you don't know for how long you will need them.

BATTERY METHOD

A good urban fire-lighting method is the battery-and-wire method, as you should have access to both of these resources. You will need two pieces of wire or a gum wrapper and a battery. Attach one wire to the positive end of the battery and one wire to the negative end. When you bring the two wires close together, a spark will jump between them. If you can place your tinder between the wires, you should be able to light it from the spark. Steel wool is an excellent tinder for this method.

Having light at night will also be an issue. I encourage you not to keep lanterns and flashlights on, to conserve your batteries in case you need them for future emergencies. A candle will provide a comforting light if you need it, but be sure to never leave a candle burning unattended. Putting the candle inside a glass jar will give it some stability and prevent the wind from blowing it out. Again, these are finite resources, so try to sleep and conserve energy during the night rather than doing activities that require light.

BRICK ROCKET STOVE

If you do not have a cooking stove in your go bag or a gas grill at home, you will need to find some method of cooking food. A brick rocket stove allows you to get the maximum heat from the minimum firewood. Simply make a small, two-foot-high chimney of bricks (one brick width per side), making sure that you leave a gap at the bottom. Place the fire at the base of the chimney and feed it with small twigs and sticks. The fire will funnel up the bricks and allow you to cook on top.

We are so used to modifying our surrounding temperature with the flick of a switch that we are no longer adapted to extreme temperatures or able to cope when we cannot avoid them. Many people die in their homes in unseasonably warm weather if their electricity gets shut off or if they don't have a decent cooling system set up. Some ways you can cool down without electricity include to:

- Limit time in the sun.

- Stay hydrated.

- Find or create shade.

- Wear light, loose-fitting cotton clothing.

- Seal off the hottest rooms in the house, and avoid them.

- Sleep downstairs or in the basement.

- Open windows at night when it is cooler, and close them during the day.

- Keep curtains closed during the day.

- Minimize opening and closing outside doors.

- Use rechargeable battery-operated fans.

- Wet a bandanna, and cover your face and neck.

- Dampen wrists and ankles.

- Refrain from cooking inside.

If you are still struggling to cool down, go to a place that you know will be cooler, such as a shopping mall (if it is open) or the local pool or swimming area.

▶ URBAN SAFETY

In disaster scenarios, people usually take one of two roads: they band together, or they develop an "every man for himself" attitude. Building a community of people who have your back will aid in ensuring your safety and
survival. It will enable you to pool resources, both physically and mentally,
and potentially barter for items you may not have. Having a good relation-
ship with your neighbors prior to finding yourself in a survival scenario will
help with this.

It is important to have your shelter out of sight and your resources stored
in a locked area, if at all possible. Do not draw attention to where you
are staying and to the fact that you have resources that may help others
through this time of disaster. Fortify your shelter or house in any way you
can. This may mean boarding up some exits and windows, finding alternative ways of locking an area, and establishing some weapons. If you do not
have access to guns and ammunition, think outside the box. If your safety
is threatened, a wood-chopping ax, heavy hammer, and baseball bat are all
effective close-contact weapons. Keep these nearby at all times. You don't
want to be paranoid and look for an attacker around every corner, but you
are not in a position to assume that everyone is a friend. Such people might
believe that their life depends on taking what you have, and if you present
an easy target, it may be taken advantage of.

Spend your time cleaning and fixing up your home to the best of your
ability. Improving your situation will help you feel proactive and stave off
feelings of helplessness and despair.

Fuel will be at a premium during these times, so try to avoid using your car.
Save the fuel for if you need to flee or evacuate again. Move around on foot
or by bike.

It is important that you do not venture out from your base unless it is absolutely necessary. If you decide that you need to leave, try to gather a group
of people to join you. There is safety in numbers when you venture out.

Be calm, but be alert and maintain good situational awareness. Avoid any encounters that feel like they might be threatening or dangerous. Urban self-defense includes:

- **Backing down:** Do not escalate an argument; if someone is aggressive, try to defuse the situation by staying calm and moving away.

- **Don't look like a target:** Wear old clothes and carry an old bag to scavenge what you can while you are out. Predators will generally prey on those they feel are weaker than them, so do not look weak or scared, and walk as if you have a purpose.

- **Have a weapon ready:** Part of carrying a weapon is also being in the headspace to use it. If you are uncertain whether you can use a weapon to inflict harm when your life is threatened, you are better not to carry one at all. It will only end up being used against you. Understand the consequences of the weapon you carry, and visualize doing what you need to do to return home safely. Do not hesitate if your life is in danger.

- **If you can limit your exposure to others and scavenge essential resources, your chances of survival go up exponentially in an urban survival scenario.**

2.7

 RIOTS

A riot is a violent disturbance of the peace by a crowd. Riots can be as dangerous and as unpredictable as natural disasters. Thousands of people are killed in riots each year worldwide. They are usually the result of a protest. There are two different types of protests: peaceful and violent. A peaceful protest has the potential to become violent at any stage. Anytime emotional, volatile groups of people gather in large numbers, there is the possibility it may become lethal.

Whether you are a willing participant, an observer, or just a passerby, it is important to always keep an eye on crowd dynamics. A peaceful protest might be hiding violence at its core. The safest course of action is to bypass violent crowds altogether and identify points of potential danger before they erupt. Skirt around a large crowd instead of making your way through it. If you are caught in the crowd, flow with it until you can move calmly and slowly to the edge. Make your way home or to a point of safety. If you are traveling with friends or loved ones, grab hands or grip elbows to ensure you stay together.

If you have been caught up in a violent protest, avoid the following areas:

- The space between groups of people with opposing views

- The front line of protests

- Places where people have been pushed up against barricades

- Lines between protestors and law enforcement

If possible, avoid approaching law enforcement, as they will be in defensive mode and may perceive anyone moving toward them as a threat.

It is very difficult to de-escalate violence in an already-agitated crowd. It is best to:

- Avoid confrontation by keeping your head down.

- Walk away, instead of running; you do not want to draw attention to yourself.

- Not take sides; be neutral or support anyone who asks whose side you are on, and move on quickly.

- Move to the edge of the crowd.

- Seek shelter inside or on the back side of a building.

- Get to elevated ground.

Avoid confrontation by keeping your head down.

Move to the edge of the crowd.

Walk away, instead of running.

STAMPEDE

This can occur when crowd control is overwhelmed, and crushing injuries or fatal suffocation occurs. It is important to maintain control over your personal space if you get caught in a stampede. Widen your stance, bend your knees, and keep your weight above your feet. Bring your arms up to a boxing position, in order to help widen the gap between you and others and protect your head. Try to avoid being pushed to the ground, as it is very difficult to get up again once you have been pushed down by a crowd of panicking people. Try to move to the edges of the crowd, as there is less pressure and force there. If you do get knocked down, assume a defensive position with your knees bent, your body curled over your knees, and your arms protecting your head until there is a gap in the crowd big enough to find your feet again.

Widen your stance.

Bring arms up to a boxing position.

If knocked down, assume defensive postion with knees bent and arms protecting your head.

Riots most commonly happen on the streets and out in public, so move to a safe, enclosed area. Lock doors and windows and stay away from them. Move to rooms that do not directly lead to the outside, and look for at least two exits in case you need to get out. Stay informed by listening to the local news or following social media, and stay in place until the danger has passed.

If you are in a vehicle:

- **Stay in the car.**

- **Keep driving as calmly as possible; do not stop to assess the situation.**

- **If someone tries to block your car, honk and keep driving toward them at a moderate speed; do not hit them if they do not give way, but be assertive.**

- **Do not let a few angry people stop you from driving.**

- **Keep going unless you absolutely can't.**

As with all dangerous scenarios, prevention is better than having to deal with a life-threatening scenario, so observe locally enforced curfews and regulations, and if you feel like tensions are mounting, calmly but quickly exit the crowd and make your way home.

LOOTING

A by-product of riots can be looting. This is the act of stealing or taking goods by force in the middle of a crisis. It is an illegal act, and usually looters don't take items of necessity but luxury items. Do not get dragged along with the crowd momentum to think this is an act of survival. Scavenging and looting are two very different actions. One comes with a penalty of fines or imprisonment after the excitement has settled, and the other is accepted if the items of value have no clear ownership, (such as supplies that are found in an abandoned or burnt-out store), and they will sustain your life.

2.8

▶ TERRORIST ATTACKS

These are violent, criminal acts committed by individuals or Predicting of where these acts may occur is almost impossible, and so your ability to prepare is minimal.

Communities can defeat terrorist attacks by looking for anything out of the ordinary and reporting it to authorities straightaway. This includes:

1. **People in stationary vehicles watching public areas or buildings for long periods of time**

2. **Vehicles moving slowly near public buildings or monuments**

3. **People using cameras or making notes of security movements**

4. **Suspicious-looking people examining entry and exits points to public buildings**

5. **People loitering for no apparent reason**

6. **People asking suspicious questions about the operations of buildings or monuments**

7. **Anyone in restricted areas without permission**

"See something, say something" has foiled planned terrorist attacks and saved thousands of lives.

If you are living in or traveling to areas of civil unrest, you should have an emergency plan organized in case you get caught up in acts of terror. This would include establishing a meeting place for your loved ones and traveling companions and making sure you have everyone's number and emergency contacts.

If an act of terrorism occurs near you:

- Try to stay calm.

- Administer medical care to yourself first and then others, if needed.

- Leave the area as soon as possible for your home or a safe space.

- Walk but do not run, unless there is an active shooter.

- Follow the advice of local authorities.

- Listen to the news for up-to-date information on action required.

- Contact friends and relatives to let them know you are okay.

EVACUATION

If you are asked to leave your home due to a terrorist attack, you will need to leave immediately, and you should:

- Change into long sleeves and pants, and put on with sturdy shoes; this clothing will act as protection if you need to have bare skin covered for any reason.

- Grab your go bag (see page 22).

- Lock up your home.

- Go where authorities say; don't use shortcuts or think you know better.

After a terrorist attack, it is important to band together with your community to help and heal. These are shocking events that have the potential to divide nations, but if you allow them to force you to live in fear, they have won. Repair, rebuild, and come back stronger.

2.9

▶ ACTIVE SHOOTER

In the United States, terrorist attacks tend to be gunfire rather than suicide vests or pipe bombs. If you encounter an active shooter, you should:

1. Immediately duck down to a squat or to hands and knees.

2. Establish the location of the shooter and move in the opposite direction.

3. Move to an area of cover, if you are not already behind cover. Cover is defined as an area that will stop or slow down bullets, like concrete walls or solid objects. Things like curtains may prevent the shooter from seeing you but will not stop bullets, so they are not a good choice.

4. Run from cover to cover to get to safety. If there is no cover available, run in a zigzag pattern, as it is harder to hit.

5. Hide somewhere you can lock and barricade the entrances. Stay clear of the doors when locating yourself inside this room. Shooters will often shoot through doors, as they tend to be the most penetrable surface available.

Remember to always look for an escape route. In the heat of the moment, you can feel trapped in a situation that you aren't actually trapped in, because of panic. People have died from being shot while huddled up against glass windows that they could have broken to escape through long before the shooter made their way to them. Just because something isn't traditionally thought of as an exit doesn't mean you can't break your way out to safety if you have to.

If all else fails, you may need to stand and fight. Team up, find any weapons or improvised weapons you can, and fight hard and with aggression. Your life may depend upon it.

Simply put: run, hide, fight.

Establish the location of the shooter and move in the opposite direction.

Move to an area of cover.

Run from cover to cover to get to safety.

2.10

▶ PANDEMICS

A pandemic is defined as an outbreak of a new disease that becomes prevalent in a country or across the world. There are usually a number of fatalities associated with pandemics. It is hard to predict when a pandemic will occur or whom it will affect.

Some things you can do to prepare for a pandemic are to:

- Learn how diseases spread, to help protect yourself and others. Viruses can spread from person to person, from a nonliving object to a person, and by people who may be infected but don't have any symptoms.

- Gather supplies—such as cleaning supplies, nonperishable foods, feminine hygiene products, prescriptions, bottled water, and food for pets—in case you need to stay home for several days or weeks; buy supplies slowly to ensure that everyone has the opportunity to buy what they need.

- Stock up on disinfectant wipes, hand sanitizer, gloves, and masks.

- Ensure you have some form of inside entertainment, including books and games.

- Make sure your go bag is stocked.

One of the reasons people end up panic buying is there tends to be denial about how a virus could have a large and lasting impact on society. Many people think it won't affect them. They do not bother preparing for it when they have plenty of time and resources, and then find themselves nervous about their supplies at the last minute. This is an example of when you need to hope for the best but prepare for the worst.

DISINFECTANT WIPES

CLEANING SPRAY

HAND SANITIZER

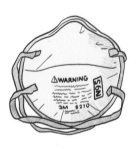

⚠WARNING
3M 8210
N95

Rx

RICE

PASTA

If you do end up in the last-minute crowds, it is important to prioritize what you should be putting in your shopping cart. Any nonperishable food items will take priority over luxury items such as toilet paper. You need to be thinking about food, water, shelter, and fire even when you are still able to go out shopping. Toilet paper, although nice to have, can be replaced by any number of other options, such as a bidet, newspaper, or tissues. (But remember to only flush toilet paper, because it can be hard to get a plumber to visit in a pandemic if you clog up the system.)

DURING A PANDEMIC

It is important to listen to what your health authorities have to say during a pandemic. There is a lot of misinformation and fearmongering that can take place, so check the sources of your information before trusting it as fact.

Some things that can help prevent the spread of a pandemic:

- **Stay home as much as possible.**

- **Cover coughs and sneezes.**

- **In public, wear a mask that covers your nose and mouth.**

- **Wash hands often with soap and water.**

- **Use hand sanitizer.**

- **Clean and disinfect high-touch objects and surfaces often.**

- **Keep six feet away from people who aren't in your household.**

- **If you have symptoms or believe you may have been exposed to the virus, contact your nearest testing site.**

- **If you do get sick, isolate so you don't pass on the virus to friends and loved ones; seek medical care if necessary.**

- **Know that it is normal to feel anxious or stressed, and talk to someone if you need help.**

- **Stay connected to friends and loved ones via virtual communication.**

AFTER A PANDEMIC

Continue taking protective actions:

- Stay home when you are sick (except to get medical care).

- Follow the guidance of your health care provider.

- Cover coughs and sneezes.

- Wash your hands with soap and water often.

▶ FORTIFYING YOUR HOME

The more difficult your home is to penetrate, the more likely a criminal will choose an easier target. There are some simple solutions that will increase your safety and help you protect your family. They include:

SECURITY CAMERAS There are many different types of cameras, ranging from quite cheap ones that can be set up with relative ease to more complicated ones that will require a company to install. You can choose to have some scattered around the house or focusing on the main entry point. Anything is better than nothing, and simply knowing that they may be caught committing a crime on camera will be enough to deter some criminals.

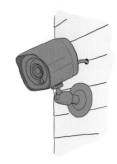

MOTION SENSOR LIGHTS It has been proven that motion-triggered lights deter many would-be intruders, and they are cheap and simple to install. They can be bought from a hardware store and placed at outside entry points. Be aware that they can be triggered by all motion, so having a dog in the backyard at night or large branches in the sensors' range on a windy night may continually set them off. It may take some experimenting to get the positioning right for you.

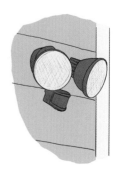

FORTIFY YOUR HOME'S ENTRY POINTS Thirty-four percent of intruders enter a house through the front door. Most of the time it was unlocked, but other times the door was kicked in. Make sure to lock your front door, especially at night. Install good security screen doors and safety chains, with double locks on the main door. Some intruders will knock to make sure no one is home. Always keep the screen door locked, so that, if you answer the door, you have one line of defense between you and a possible home invader.

SECURE YOUR WINDOWS The next-most-common entry points are windows. Make sure that your windows have locks and that you use them. Window alarms work when the intruder slides the window but not when they break them. A simple way to fortify them is security window film. It's a transparent film that makes windows harder to break or shatter.

BELLS OR CHIMES Install them on your doors so that they are set off whenever the door is opened or closed. If you know that you are alone in the house and you hear the sound, you know to take action to deal with an intruder.

DOGS When interviewed, most thieves say they would be deterred if a house had a large dog in residence. This should never be a reason to get a dog, as they require care and attention, but if you love dogs and have the time to care for them, they can help keep intruders away.

TREES AND SHRUBS These are a long-term plan, as they will take time to grow once planted, but if people can't see the target, they will be less temped to rob it.

CACTUSES Planted under your first-floor windows, they will prevent would-be intruders from breaking and entering in these locations, due to the painful, prickly barrier these plants present.

WEAPONS What type of weapon you have in your house will depend on the laws in your country, but arming yourself and making sure you are educated to competently use your weapon of choice will allow you to protect yourself if all else has failed.

Urban survival is all about your ability to survive a widespread disaster while remaining in a densely populated urban environment. You will need all your survival attitudes to help yourself and others through these often life-changing events, remaining positive and adaptable while being proactive to make the situation better for everyone. One step at a time, one job at a time, make today better than yesterday to rebuild your future.

3

Basic Needs

THE DIFFERENCE BETWEEN A WANT AND A NEED is that a need is something that if you don't have it, you will eventually die. A want is everything else. In urban survival scenarios, shelter is often not as imperative as in wilderness survival. In the wake of natural disasters or other urban disasters the basic needs in a survival situation are:

Water • Food • Fire • Shelter

3.1

▶ **WATER**

Water makes up about 70 percent of our body. It circulates through the blood and is responsible for transporting essential nutrients and oxygen to our organs. It then takes the toxins and waste from those organs and gets it out of our bodies in the form of sweat and urine. Basically, if you don't drink enough water, you are not getting good things to your organs and cells, and you aren't getting bad things out of your body.

What is enough water? Everyone has their own thoughts on this topic, and it ranges from two liters a day to six liters a day. Even scientists have trouble agreeing on this one, as every person's water needs are different, depending on such things as their height, weight, gender, and propensity to sweat, and even the different ways an individual processes water.

Personally, I work on three liters a day, but I have survived for twenty-one days on less than a liter a day with no lasting adverse side effects.

Dehydration occurs when your body loses more fluids than it consumes. Most people don't consume enough water, and when dehydration symptoms occur, we often misdiagnose them and combat them with diuretics (tea or coffee) and medication that can further exacerbate the problem.

(opposite) Digging for water; see page 136.

Next time you exhibit any of the following symptoms, try drinking a big glass of water and waiting for ten minutes to see if it helps.

Dehydration symptoms include:

- Dry mouth

- Tiredness or fatigue

- Thirst

- Lack of urination (you should be peeing once every few hours)

- Dark-colored urine

- Headache

- Dizziness

If untreated, dehydration can progress into foggy thinking, the inability to make rational decisions, and eventually seizures, brain damage, and death.

It is largely accepted that you can live approximately three days without water, but this can change rapidly, depending on your circumstances. If it is hot, you can die without water in less than a day. If you are exerting a large amount of effort and sweating a lot, you may last less than that. Even if it is cold and windy, you may be losing more moisture than you think.

Ways to prevent water loss:

- **Don't exert yourself.**

- **Keep cool; stay in the shade where possible.**

- **Do not lie on hot ground.**

- **Keep talking to a minimum.**

- **Don't eat, or eat very little, as digestion requires water.**

My first rule about water: always carry more water than you think you will need. It is your most precious resource. All your other equipment won't mean anything if you can't get enough water.

If we are sticking to the rule of threes, where we agree that we can last three minutes without oxygen, three hours in extreme cold, and three days without water, then water quickly becomes a priority after making sure that we can shelter ourselves sufficiently to stay warm.

There are many different methods of sourcing and purifying water. I will go into greater detail in the climate sections for ones that are specific to locations, but in this section, I will discuss the most successful and popular methods that can be utilized in most areas. I will divide the purification into techniques that don't require any specialized equipment, and also popular ones that rely on you being prepared the moment that an outdoor trip turns into a survival scenario.

Vegetation can provide water.

▶ FINDING WATER

- **Collect rainfall** If you happen to be in a location that does get some rain, your best bet for collecting pure, drinkable water is from the sky. Craft containers out of anything you can find. There is a lot of garbage in the world, so if you can find old water bottles or cans, cut the top off and use large leaves to funnel the water into these vessels. Get creative. Bamboo cut in half can work as gutters on your shelter and can direct water into bamboo containers. Bark works just as well. Natural divots in rocks will catch water in pools, and some plants catch water at the base of their leaves. A rainstorm can be a great asset if you are prepared for it.

- **Observe vegetation** Vegetation cannot grow without a water source; however, some desert plants have adapted to survive with very little. If you can get to a high point, try to locate an area where the vegetation grows larger, lusher, and greener than its surroundings. This is a good indicator that water may be in that area.

- **Dig for water** Look for damp mud or soil patches, and dig there. Soon your hole should start to fill with muddy water. Allow the sediment to settle before drinking. You can also drain the water through your clothing if you are in desperate need. If there are no moist patches, try digging on the outside of the bends in a dry riverbed. When the river did have surface water, these areas were where it was slowest moving, so water is more likely to have seeped into the underlying ground. You may need to dig for over a foot before water appears. If it hasn't appeared by then, try a hole in another location.

- **Look at the landscape** Water always flows downhill, so lower-lying areas and valleys are a good place to look if there are not obvious areas of vegetation.

- **Observe animal tracks** Most animals need water to survive as much as we do and, over the course of days, will make their way to the closest water source to slake their thirst. Well-worn animal paths are a good indication that water is nearby. Animals may be scattered to feed, but

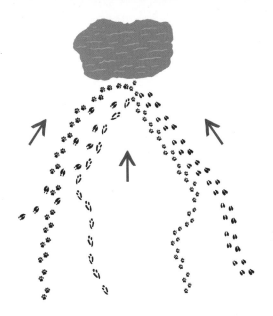

their paths will merge on the way to water, creating an arrow-like pattern to guide you. It's a good idea to note if the tracks are fresh, because animal paths may stay obvious for a long time in dry areas after the water source has dried up. It might also take a moment to figure out which direction to travel, but following the arrow pattern will give you a good indication as soon as a fork in the road is discovered. One major exception to this rule is reptiles. They don't require a water source, as they are able to access enough water to survive from dew and their food. So following snakes and lizards, especially in a desert setting, probably won't help you at all.

- **Bird behavior** A lot of seed-eating birds require a drink every day, so observing bird flight patterns can also be a good indicator of water. If the birds are flying in a tight formation or line, they are generally heading toward water. If they are flying in a wide, more relaxed formation, they are generally flying away from water. It's also good to note that smaller birds need to be closer to a water source, so finding smaller birds such as wrens and bee-eaters is a good sign.

- **Insect activity** Bees are a great indication of water nearby, although they will travel up to two and a half miles to get it if they need to. Many types of wasps also require a water source nearby, as they build their nests predominantly out of mud. Keeping an eye out for the direction bees and wasps are traveling may give you some idea of a direction to travel if your water situation is dire.

3.1.2

▶ COLLECTING WATER

Most of these methods involve having some kind of plastic bag or plastic sheet with you in order to collect water. They also require you to be in an area where there is an abundance of green leafy trees. The first method works well in desert conditions, where you have hot days but clear, cooler nights, and requires no plastic.

- **DEW COLLECTING** Dew forms as temperatures drop and objects cool down. This forces water vapor in the air around cooling objects to condense. This then collects on the objects. Leaving clothing outside at night may result in being able to wring out some moisture in the morning. Tying clothing around your legs and walking through the grass and bushes will also transfer this moisture to your clothes, and you should be able to wring out enough to keep you sated.

- **LEAF CONDENSATION** If you have a clear plastic bag of any sort, then this method is a good way to collect drinking water. It is a passive collection method, meaning that you don't have to do much work to gain the water. This is important, keeping in mind that some methods of procuring water can burn more water than they obtain.

In the early morning, place a small stone in the bottom of the plastic bag and wrap your bag around a bunch of leaves on a tree branch. You need to choose a branch that extends beyond the main canopy; you are looking for one that will be in full sun during the day. Tie the top of the bag tight around the branch, and leave it over the course of the day. If the area is heavily wooded, you may need to change the branch halfway through the day if it becomes covered in shade.

Water naturally travels from the trunk of the tree to the leaves, where it transpires into the air. Covering the leaves with the bag means this water condenses in the plastic and will collect in the bottom of the bag. You may want to swap branches and leaf bundles as the day progresses to ensure a constant supply.

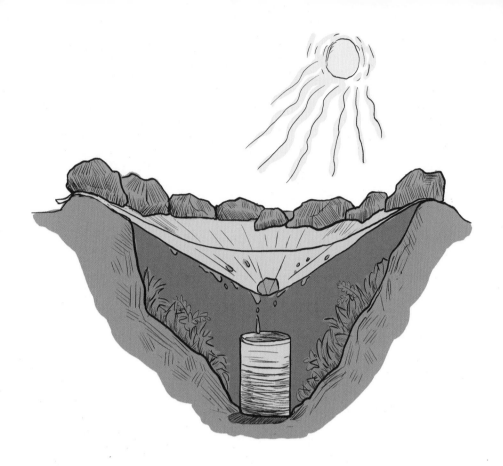

- **SOLAR STILL** This method of water collection will require a clear plastic sheet and a container to collect water in. Dig a hole about three feet long and a foot deep in a place that gets the most sun throughout the day. Place the container in the center of the hole, and surround it with green leafy material. The fleshier the vegetation, the more moisture it is likely to contain. Place the plastic sheet over the hole, making sure that you seal the sides. Place a stone in the center of the sheet, so that it forms a low point in the plastic over the container. The sun will cause the moisture to evaporate from the vegetation and condensate on the plastic, where it will form drops of pure, drinkable water that will slide into the waiting container.

This method can be used to distill the salt out of seawater and the impurities out of urine. It can also be used where the ground is moist but not puddling, to draw the moisture out of wet soil.

- **SALTWATER STILL** There are many different and complex ways to desalinate salt water. The basic idea is that you need to heat the salt water so that the pure water rises from it as steam. This steam then needs to be collected and cooled in such a way that it reverts to liquid form, this time without the salt in it. If you have a complex array of pipes and collection pots and perhaps some duct tape, you could rig up an efficient system to keep many people satisfied with drinking water indefinitely. However, this is a lot of equipment to rely on having, and you can achieve a smaller version of this with a clear water bottle and a can. You won't be able to process as much water at a time, but it will help to keep you alive.

Cut the bottom off the water bottle and the top off the can. Fold the bottom sides of the water bottle up into itself to create a gutter to catch the desalinated water. Fill the can with salt water, and place it inside of the water bottle. Make sure the lid is on the water bottle, and place your still in the full sun. The water will evaporate from the can in the heat and re-form on the inside of the water bottle, sliding down the sides to be caught in the gutter. This method takes time and sunny weather, so make sure you set this up way before dehydration sets in. If possible, make multiple setups.

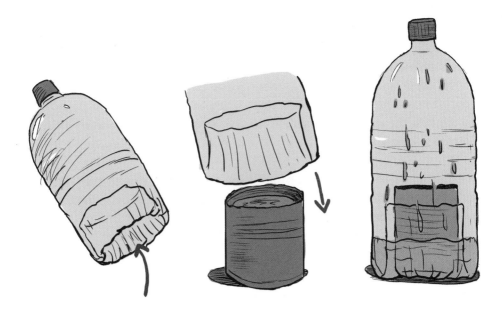

▶ PURIFICATION TECHNIQUES

If you are ever asking yourself about whether you need to purify ground-water before you drink it, the answer is yes. Ninety percent of the world's groundwater is polluted in some way, including from chemicals, bacteria, viruses, parasites, or salts. And that pollution may not be obvious. The idea of drinking clear, bubbly, running water may be more appealing than drinking out of a muddy puddle, but you never know what is upstream from you. If something has died in a lovely pool and its rotting bacteria is floating down that clear, cool water, it will make you very sick. Always purify water if you can.

This is where I need you to get flexible with your thinking. If not drinking that water WILL lead to your death but drinking it MIGHT save your life, drink the water. Just exhaust all other options first.

Most water pollutants will act as poison in your body. When your body is poisoned, it wants to purge the poison out, and it does so by making you vomit, sweat, and have diarrhea. These are all things that quickly dehydrate your body and hasten you toward death if you can't replenish your fluids. By drinking the water, you may feel like you are saving your life when in fact you are ending it faster.

It is crucial for you to remember that if you drink water without purifying it, you run the risk of becoming sick. If you have any way of purifying the water, do so before consuming.

(opposite, above) Purification by straining; see page 144.
(opposite, below) Purification by boiling; see page 148.

BASIC NEEDS

▶ WATER PURIFICATION—WITHOUT GEAR

- **STRAINING** The absolute minimum you should do with murky water is to strain it. It also should be the start of any other technique if your water has chunks in it. This simply involves passing it through some clothing so that the larger impurities are filtered out. This only removes floating particulates; it doesn't take out any poisons.

- **WATER WELL** This water-straining technique is often referred to as a gypsy well. It's simply the method of digging a hole a few yards from a murky water source and allowing the ground to do the filtering for you. If you are there for a while, you can line the well with sticks to prevent the sides from falling in. Over time, all sediment should sink to the bottom, leaving you with clear water to drink. Just remember, this is an emergency water source and can't be trusted not to contain impurities.

  This method can also be tried on the coast to source fresh water by the ocean. Dig a hole behind the first layer of sand dunes above the high tide mark. The sand hills trap rainwater behind them, and it tends to float on top of the denser layer of salt water beneath it. The hole only needs to be deep enough to expose the first inch or so of water; otherwise, salt water will flood in and pollute the fresh water.

- **STRAINING WITH CHARCOAL** If you are unable to get a fire burning to purify your water but have had a fire in the past or happen to be in an area that a bushfire has swept through, you can use the fire's by-product of charcoal to fashion a homemade water filter. This should not be your first choice, as it may not be completely effective, but it is better than sucking the water straight out of the stream or puddle. Simply crush up the charcoal and layer it in the fabric you are straining through. Charcoal has the amazing property of being able to absorb toxins from water.

  Charcoal is also a good remedy for upset stomachs and bloating. Crumble it into a powder, and mix it with water. Ingest it to help eliminate toxins, if you suspect you have consumed something that may have poisoned your system.

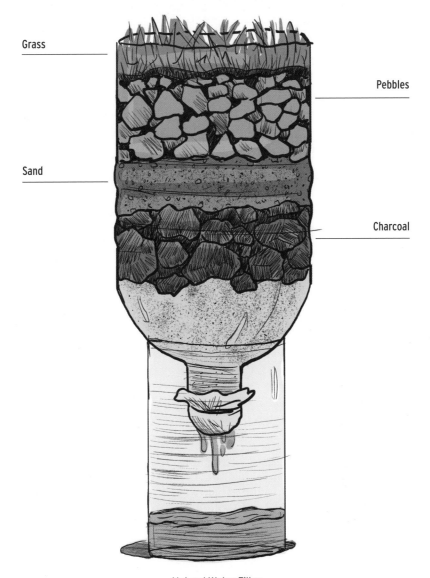

Grass

Pebbles

Sand

Charcoal

Natural Water Filter

- **NATURAL WATER FILTER** In an open-ended container, place alternating layers of pebbles, sand, grass, and charcoal. It works best when the container tapers to a smaller end. Passing the water through the pebbles, sand, and grass will remove the sediment from the water, and the charcoal should kill any bacteria.

  The container can be created with bamboo or flexible strips of bark.

What if you don't have a container?

The answer to this is the hot-rock boiling technique. You will need a fire for this method, but other than that, all you need is a waterproof vessel (a large bamboo stem or bark bowl works nicely) and some rocks a little smaller than your fist. Place the rocks in the fire to heat them up. If you have some plastic, you can also dig a pit, line it with plastic, and fill the pit with water. Place the hot rocks into this pit, making sure that you do not get the rocks on dry plastic.

Be aware that river rocks have the tendency to explode, due to tiny pockets of air or water trapped in them that expand when heated. This can be dangerous, with small, hot shards showering in all directions.

Once the rocks are red hot, use two sticks to pull them out of the fire and put them in the water in your vessel. You may need to repeat this several times to get a rolling boil, but eventually the rocks will boil the water.

3.1.3.2

▶ WATER PURIFICATION—WITH GEAR

Assuming that you were prepared when you headed into the outdoors or a disaster struck, here are some of the more popular ways to purify water:

- **BOILING** Boiling is the most effective way of making your water fit to drink. That's why a pot or steel cup is always in my top-four items to bring into a survival scenario. If you have something to boil water in and a fire, then you can make water safe to drink. Bringing the water to a rolling boil (where the bubbles are continuously moving from the bottom of the water to the top) will kill any bacteria, viruses, or parasites that could make you sick.

If you don't have a pot to boil water in, it is possible to boil water in a plastic container. Don't put the plastic container directly on the fire, as the plastic will melt; but if you can suspend the bottle above the fire, the water will boil before the plastic melts. This is because the melting point of plastic is higher than the boiling point of water. This is not an ideal method of water purification, as heating the plastic releases carcinogens into the water, but it will save your life, so it is worth doing for the short term. Keep in mind that you may not see bubbling when the water is at the boiling point due to the lid being on the bottle, so keep an eye out for small bubbles forming on the bottom to indicate it has reached that stage.

- **WATER FILTER** There are many water filters on the market, and they are a great way of removing impurities from your water source. They usually work by either a pumping action or gravity, and send the water over a filter designed to specifically remove impurities from water. They can purify large amounts of water quickly and can last years when maintained correctly. They are a great asset to carry in your pack, as they will allow you to carry less water if you know you will come across water sources.

- **LIFE STRAW** This is the smaller version of a water filter. The advantage of the straw is that it is lighter and smaller but is really designed for emergency use only. It works as a normal straw does, so you can only drink what you can take in at the time, whereas a larger filter allows you to pump enough to store for later.

- **WATER PURIFICATION TABLETS** These tablets typically contain chlorine, chlorine dioxide, or iodine. These chemicals deactivate bacteria, viruses, and parasites and make the water safe to drink. They usually require some kind of resting period between putting in the water and being able to drink. Make sure that you always follow the instructions, and be aware that they are not necessarily good for your body with long-term use.

  Iodine is commonly found in first aid kits, as it is great for disinfecting cuts. It can also be used to clean your water, but it can leave it tasting strange. A good rule of thumb is five to ten drops per liter, leave for five minutes, and then drink. Iodine is not recommended for people with thyroid issues, so use other methods if this applies to you.

Finally, **never drink your own urine**. This theory has been made popular by a famous survivalist, but very rarely works. If you are going to drink your own pee, it needs to be before you are dehydrated, when your pee is a majority water rather than full of toxic waste products. Usually, people resort to drinking their own pee when the situation has gotten dire and they are so thirsty that they see no other option. By then, their urine is dark and full of toxins and bacteria that the kidneys have filtered out. Introducing this back into your system leads to you becoming more dehydrated and stresses your kidneys, which can cause them to shut down. This leads to you dying faster than you would have without drinking the pee.

If your life depends upon it and you have no way to purify the water you have found, drink sparingly the clearest, most rapidly flowing water you can find.

3.2

▶ **FIRE**

There are many reasons why fire is in the basic needs section of survival. It contributes to all the other basic needs in some way and adds so much more to your survival on its own. Fire will help you survive longer than three hours in exposed conditions, it is one of the best methods of purifying your water to make it potable, and it can make the food you have found safer and more palatable to eat. It can also help keep large predators and insects at bay and signal for help. It is one of the essentials that may make the difference between you surviving and not.

There is one thing that all animals fear: fire. With the exception of the fire-fighting rhinoceros in Africa, most animals will avoid the heat of a flame. In a survival situation, make it a priority to have a fire burning before the sun sets, and make sure you have enough wood stockpiled to ensure that the fire is kept burning throughout the night. The fire doesn't need to be a big one. In most cases, simply the smell of the wood burning will be an ample deterrent.

Fires are also great for morale. They add a feeling of warmth and safety in a situation that can otherwise feel out of control and scary.

There are many methods for getting a fire going in the outdoors. Almost every group of Indigenous people had a different method or variation of how best to make fire in their region. This being a book about survival, not bushcraft, I am going to focus on the ones that you will most likely need to try if you are thrust into a survival situation rather than if you came prepared, although I will touch on some of the more popular man-made ones.

The key to getting a good fire going is preparation. It doesn't matter if you have fire-lighting methods on you or if you have to improvise; what you do before even making a spark, flame, or coal will be the difference between getting a roaring fire going or wasting valuable resources, energy, and time.

Some of the bonuses of having a fire include:

- Warmth

- Protection

- Signaling for rescue

- Cooking

- Psychological benefits

3.2.1

▶ FIRE PREPARATION

The three things needed to make a flame are fuel, a heat source, and oxygen.

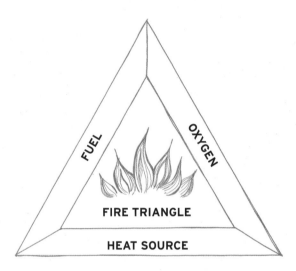

FIRE TRIANGLE

Fuel is the main thing that you need to prepare before making a heat source. I have seen many people put in a huge effort to make a friction fire coal, only to have it smolder out while they are frantically searching around for materials to ignite it in. Be aware that most methods of primitive fire making don't finish with you having a flame; they finish with you having a coal, which you then have to nurse into a flame.

A heat source will take resources or time to make. Even if you have matches or a lighter on you, be aware that these resources are finite, and make sure that you make the most of every match or strike of the lighter.

Oxygen is fortunately all around us with the air we breathe, so apart from avoiding accidentally smothering the heat source and locating the fire out of the wind, the preparation for this is minimal.

FUEL

Fire fuel can be broken down into three different types:

1. Tinder

2. Kindling

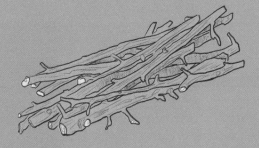

3. Fuel

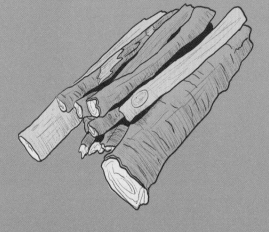

TINDER

This is any material that takes a minimal amount of heat to make it catch on fire. The key to good tinder is that it must be dry. Look for fine-grain fibers that can fluff up easily when rubbed between your hands. Its purpose is to be a coal or spark extender. This means that it should take the heat from the heat source and be able to either turn it into a flame or make a bigger, hotter coal. Some materials ignite well but burn too quickly to be useful on their own. Dry cattail heads are a good example of this. They work great when combined with other materials, but burn out too quickly on their own.

The best way to collect tinder ready for your heat source is to make a tinder bundle or bird nest. When a bird makes its nest, it has bigger materials on the outside to keep the structure of the nest and then smaller materials on the inside to protect the baby bird. The finest materials should be on the inside, ready to amp up the heat source, and the larger materials should be on the outside, ready to fuel the flame.

The outer layer of a tinder bundle should also be mostly fine, dry, combustible material. I find that dry grass tied into a knot, creating a nest for the smaller materials, works well. You can also use bark, palm fibers, or coconut husk. It's a good idea to experiment in your area to see what works for you. Some dry fibers seem like they might work but don't have the combustible properties to ensure success, so they could lead to you wasting time and energy. One of my favorite tinder finds is white punk fungus. It can be found in Australia, New Zealand, and South America, and if you send a small spark onto the fungus directly, it will catch easily and roll a coal until the whole fungus is consumed.

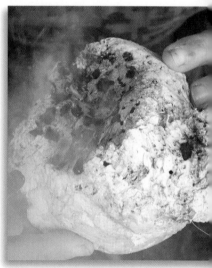

White punk fungus

The idea of a tinder bundle is that once you have your coal or heat source, you place it in the center of the bundle and fold over the edges of the bundle so the coal is touching as much fuel as possible. By firmly (but not wildly) blowing into the bundle, you add enough oxygen for that coal to ignite. This is where preparation of kindling comes in; without prior preparation, your tinder bundle will quickly burn out, and you will have to begin again.

Good inner material should almost be the consistency of fluff or dust. Things that work great for this are:

- Dry grasses or the inner bark of some trees, rubbed between your hands

- Bracket fungus pounded into a fine dust

- Palm fibers

- Cattail heads

- Dry dung from grass-eating animals, ground to a fine dust

KINDLING

This is the wood used to extend the flames of the tinder bundle into a useful fire. I always think of kindling as being the size of anything from a toothpick to a thumb. Make sure that this wood is also dry, as the tinder bundle flame won't burn long enough or hot enough to dry out wood. I discuss how to find dry wood in wet conditions in the relevant climate chapters, but for now, gather a handful of toothpick-sized wood, two handfuls of pencil-sized wood, and two handfuls of thumb-sized wood.

There are many and varied methods of setting up a fire lay (the structure made with kindling). Some people like to dig a hole to contain the fire, and others like to make a ring of stones. I do like to have some clearly defined fire area so that the fire doesn't sprawl, but that is a personal choice. Just remember that if you line your fire with rocks, you need to make sure that they are not river rocks. Wet rocks or river rocks tend to explode when heated and can cause nasty injuries. To avoid this, bang the rocks together and discard any rocks that sound hollow or are brittle.

I will give you a few different examples of log lays, but the main things to remember are:

- **Try to find a location out of the wind.**

- **Clear the area around where you intend to make your fire.**

- **Make sure the ground isn't damp, and if it is, lay down a branch platform to keep your fire base dry.**

- **Leave an area at the base of your wood pile to place your tinder bundle in; fire burns upward, so it will seek its fuel above it.**

- **Go from smaller wood to larger wood:** toothpicks at the bottom of your pile where the tinder bundle will be placed, to thumb-sized wood on top.

- **Don't pack the wood on too thickly or too thinly; too much wood will smother the flame, and too little won't provide enough fuel, and the flame will burn out.**

THE TEPEE LAY

This is exactly what the name suggests. Prop the toothpick-sized twigs on your cleared ground first, and then layer the outside of them with the pencil-sized twigs and lastly the thumb-sized branches. I make sure that I don't use all my kindling in the structure, so that I will have some to feed into the fire if I have misjudged how much of each size I will need. Your on-fire tinder bundle is then inserted beneath the toothpick- sized twigs. As the flame burns upward, it will light the toothpicks, which in turn will provide enough sustained heat to light the pencils, etc.

If you have a ready flame such as a match or lighter, you can skip the tinder-bundle stage and head straight to making the log lay. Just make sure you compensate by filling the space under the toothpick-sized twigs with some smaller, highly flammable material to get burning first.

THE LOG CABIN LAY

Again, collect your handfuls of toothpick-, pencil-, and thumb-sized twigs. You will also need two bigger pieces of wood laid out parallel to each other. Scrape out a hole to place the tinder bundle into, and lay the toothpick-sized twigs across the hole, with a handful running one way and a handful running perpendicular (at right angles) to them. The next pencil-sized layer should sit on your two parallel logs, again crisscrossing a layer each, and, finally, the same with the thumb-sized branches. With this method, you can stack your thicker fuel at the top of the cabin structure early in the fire-making process, because it won't collapse in on itself and smother the fire, as can sometimes happen if you put big wood on the tepee structure too soon.

Place the tinder bundle or flame under the toothpick-sized twigs, and you should soon have a fire.

FUEL

This is the wood that you use to keep your fire going. How well it burns will depend on where you are and the types of wood you have access to. As a general rule, hardwoods burn hotter and longer than softwoods and produce bigger coals. These are the kind of fuels you are looking for to keep your fire going through the night. The less you have to tend your fire, the better sleep you will get.

Assuming you don't have an ax or saw with you, the best way to break up these larger pieces of wood is by smacking them over a rock or bending them between two solid objects (boulders or large tree trunks work). If they are too large to break, you can either place them over the fire and let the fire burn each piece in half for you, or you can feed an end in at a time. This allows you to burn quite large logs that will sustain the fire for a good length of time, and it also conserves the energy you may burn from trying to break the wood.

Make sure you avoid the dead wood from poisonous plants such as poison oak or the stinging tree. Smoke from burning poisonous plants can be toxic and cause death or damage to lungs and eyes.

As always, you are trying to conserve energy. Do not make a massive fire unless you are trying to signal for help. A small fire will keep you just as warm if positioned properly, and it doesn't take much of a flame to boil water.

Try to find dry standing wood or wood that is off the ground, as it will generally be a more solid wood. Any wood that has sat on the ground for a while will tend to be rotten or full of termites and will burn faster than standing wood.

Make sure to collect more fuel than you think you will need. You don't want to blunder around in the dark to get more wood if your fire has gone out and you are freezing. Find a way to store wood that will keep it dry or dry it out. I often build a small shelter near the fire that houses my collected wood. I make sure that the wood is off the ground and covered. That way I'm never caught out if it rains.

If you are trying to dry wet wood, place it either around the fire or on a rack over the fire. Just make sure it is not so close that it catches on fire before you want it to.

FEATHER STICK

No fire preparation section would be complete without mentioning a feather stick. It is tinder, kindling, and fuel all in one and a popular method of starting fires, especially in adverse weather. If you make one well enough, you can even light it from a spark.

To create a feather stick, choose a straight, dry stick with no knots. Lay your blade flat on the stick and then tilt the angle of the blade slightly toward the wood. Run the blade all the way down the stick, stopping just before the bottom of the stick so that the shaving remains attached to the stick. Turn the stick around and repeat. Keep repeating until you end up with a thin stick with shavings attached. Place this inside your fire lay, and add an ignition source.

Once you have sufficient tinder, kindling, and fuel for your fire, it is time to decide how best to make your fire.

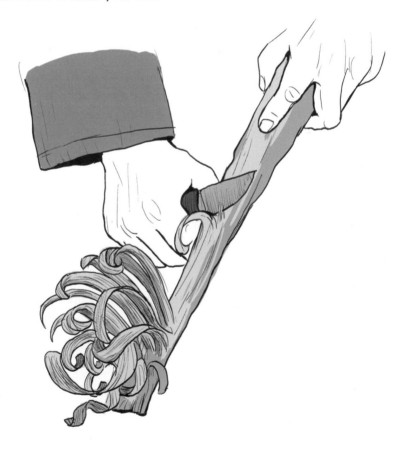

3.2.2

▶ WAYS TO MAKE FIRE

I'm sure that the first thing most people imagine when they think about making a fire in a survival situation is the friction fire method, or what's better known as rubbing two sticks together. It is a very physically demanding and technical process, and I have seen many gifted survivalists not get a fire going after hours of trying this method under pressure. Before embarking on the friction method, try one of these other techniques if you have the requisite tools—they are much simpler and will burn fewer calories.

3.2.2.1

▶ REFRACTION METHODS

One of the less strenuous methods of making a fire is to allow the sun to shine through something that will magnify the sun's heat. The most obvious is a magnifying glass. If you have one on you, that's a bonus, but there are a few ways of re-creating the effects of a magnifying glass in a survival scenario.

Human beings have managed to pollute just about everywhere in the world with our garbage, so you can usually manage to find these types of things in quite remote locations. The most obvious is a piece of glass from such things as a broken bottle or a camera lens, but a piece of a plastic bottle will work also. I have made fire using the following methods of refraction:

- Magnifying glass—your compass usually has a little one incorporated into it.

- Reading glasses—if they have a magnifying lens.

- Clear plastic water bottle—if it's filled with water, you can use the base to concentrate the sun's rays into a point.

It can also be done with a clear plastic bag full of water and a piece of ice; however, conditions must be ideal for both.

This method will not work at night for obvious reasons, and the closer the sun gets toward the horizon, the less direct heat there is. This method is best tried in the middle of the day, when the sun is at its peak. Aim the heat spot you are creating for the smallest material at the center of your tinder bundle.

3.2.2.2

▶ BATTERY METHOD

This method works if you have a flashlight or something that runs on batteries (like a camera). You will also need two pieces of wire; perhaps there is a fence nearby or the inside of an electrical cord, such as a phone charger.

Attach one wire to the positive end of the battery and one wire to the negative end. When you bring the two wires close together, a spark will jump between them. If you can place your tinder between the wires, you should be able to light it from the spark.

3.2.2.3

▶ FERRO RODS

Although this is technically a friction fire method, since the spark is caused by friction between a rod and a striker, this method needs a whole section of its own, because in the survival world it is one of the most popular yet misunderstood methods of fire making.

These handy little gadgets are often called a "flint and steel," which is not accurate to describe them but is a reflection of their past. Historically, people would hit a rock called flint with their steel knives to create a spark to make a fire. As time went by, the ferro rod was invented, combining a mixture of metal alloys into what is called mischmetal. When struck with a steel striker, this mischmetal ignites with a spark that burns hotter and longer than a spark caused by simply striking two natural rocks together, or a rock and a knife.

The problem is that many survivalists and outdoors people put these gadgets in their packs believing that they have fire sorted, when in reality they only have a method of getting a spark. The process needs to go one step further to knowing how to get the hottest, most sustained spark and what material will ignite with that spark. I have seen many people aiming their ferro rod at a bundle of twigs and wondering why nothing is igniting.

The best way to use a ferro rod is to position the rod so it is facing low and central to your tinder. In the hand holding the striker, brace your knuckles on the ground or your shoe and then sharply pull back the hand with the ferro rod in it. The striker should be at about a 30-degree angle to the rod for best results. If you push the striker toward the bundle, you risk displacing your tinder before the spark reaches it. As with any survival kit, if you choose to have a ferro rod in your bag, make sure you know how to use it and what tinder ignites best with a spark in your area or the area you're visiting.

3.2.2.4

▶ PERCUSSION FIRE METHODS

All around the world, there are rocks that will create a spark when hit off each other or off a knife with a high carbon content. The spark is generally cooler and faster burning than one produced by a ferro rod, so it is essential to have a good, flammable tinder bundle ready. This method saved my life when I was racing *First Man Out* survivalist Ed Stafford out of a high-altitude mountain pass in Sichuan Province in China. We spent a fair amount of our time above the snow line, and just below the snow line was mostly rain-soaked wood, not ideal for friction fire. I knew that pyrite was native to that area and kept my eye out for some among the thick rockpiles on the edges of the mountain streams. I was lucky enough to find some with a high iron content and was able to get a spark into some dried and ground-up chaga fungus. This created a coal that I could make a fire out of. The weather got down to below -25°F that night, and I would have died had I not been able to get a fire going.

As previously noted, the technique was popularly known as the flint-and-steel method. This is because flint is found in most places in the world, and it dependably produces good sparks when hit with a high-carbon-content metal. Flint tends to be a chalky-looking, fine-grained rock that is either light gray or white in color if you can find it, but most fine-grained rocks that can be broken to have a sharp edge will usually work if flint isn't readily available.

If you are unsure about how to identify flint, try a variety of rocks lying around to see if one produces a spark. Even if you can't see the spark, sometimes you will smell a distinctive match smell on the rocks after striking. You have to hit the rock quite hard and sharply to get the spark, but once you get the hang of it, it's an easy and reliable fire-lighting method.

Quartz also works with a metal striker, and its white color makes it fairly easy to identify.

The only stone that I have found that will deliver a workable spark when struck off itself is iron pyrite. This is less readily found around the world, but there is evidence that some of the most primitive cultures carried with them pieces of this rock specifically to make fire with.

Pyrite

Flint

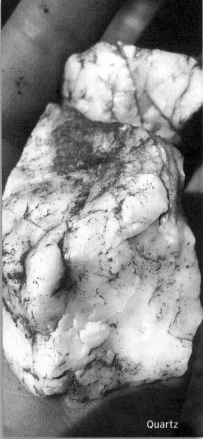

Quartz

3.2.2.5

▶ FRICTION FIRE METHODS

There are many different forms of friction fire, but they all usually involve rapidly rubbing two pieces of wood together to create enough heat and dust to make a hot coal. I would recommend learning one or some of these techniques before you take off on your extreme outdoor adventure, because they are very difficult to learn on the fly. However, necessity is the mother of invention, so if you understand the theory behind what works and what doesn't, you may be able to make it work if your life depends on it.

There are certain woods that work better for friction fire making than others. Rather than having you learn all the best friction fire woods in the world, I am going to give you a set of properties to look for that work best:

- Dry

- Soft, lightweight wood—but not punky or rotten

- Sourced from faster-growing trees or weeds

- Straight—free from bends or knots

It is better if you choose a slightly softer piece of wood for your spindle with a slightly harder piece of wood for your baseboard, but wood of the same density will work too.

Over the years, I have made friction fires with types of wood that people have told me will not work, so don't get hung up on what someone else has told you; try everything for yourself. One of the most important things to remember is that both bits of wood must be bone dry. Any dampness in either will probably result in failure. Be aware of how damp the ground you are working on is. Any moisture on the ground will be absorbed into the drier wood and lead to a lack of success as well.

With most of these methods, you will need a notch to keep your spindle or drill piece moving in the same place. This will be a hole for the hand drill and bow drill methods and a horizontal notch for the fire saw and fire plow methods. You will also need a catchment area for the "dust" you produce.

This dust will be the main indicator of how well your method is working. It needs to be a dark brown, almost-black color. If your dust is light in color, you either need to change the pressure of the strokes or the speed of the strokes, usually increasing it rather than decreasing it. This dust is what will combust to form a coal, so make sure it doesn't blow away or fall out of the notch.

This can be a very physically demanding way to get a fire going, so start slowly with your strokes. With the right amount of pressure, you can get heat without rapid movement. As smoke starts to be seen, increase the pace of your strokes and for longer than you think.

Once you have a smoking coal, take your time and transfer it to your tinder bundle. You will have created an excess of dust that will help the coal increase its size over a minute or so, which means you don't have to rush.

These are just the basics of friction fire methods. Each method has different specifics that I will outline further in the following pages. If you are unsure if a wood will work, just give it a go. If the wood heats up, changes color, or produces dust or smoke, it is worth putting in a bit of effort with.

HAND DRILL

This is the simplest of friction fire methods, given that it only needs two pieces of wood. It is also one of the hardest methods, because it requires fairly specific wood types and some good upper-body strength to be successful. You will need a straight, thin spindle about a foot and a half long with a half-inch diameter and a baseboard about three-quarters of an inch thick. Carve one end of the spindle into an arch. The arched side rests on the baseboard.

Carve a divot into the baseboard to keep the spindle in place, and place your hands flat on either side of the spindle. When you first start learning this technique, you will need to anchor the baseboard in place with your foot. Push your hands together, and spin the spindle with a downward pressure to help generate the heat required. If you are creating enough friction, the baseboard will start to smoke, and you will burn a circle into the baseboard. Using a sharp edge, cut a notch into the side of the baseboard, making the circle look like Pac-Man. Place a leaf or a piece of bark under the notch to catch your dust. Repeat the spinning motion until the notch fills up with black dust and begins to smoke. With enough heat and friction, this dust will ignite into a coal.

This action of burning in a hole, cutting a notch, and filling the notch with dust is consistent with both the strap drill and bow drill methods as well.

STRAP DRILL

This personally is one of my favorite methods of friction fire making. It is also one of the friction fire methods that requires the least amount of strength or exertion, and I have seen children as young as five master it. This method requires only two additional pieces of equipment from the hand drill, but it is a two-person method, so if you are flying solo, then it's not the method for you.

You will need a piece of rope or cordage and a bearing block. I have used a shoelace for this method, so if you are wearing laced shoes, then you are in luck. If you are not and do not have any ready-made cord with you, make natural cordage (see page 214). The cord only needs to be as long as a shoelace. The bearing block needs to have a hole or divot in it. If you are using wood, the wood needs to be of a harder wood than the spindle. You can use bone, antler, rocks, or shells for your bearing block. As long as the spindle can spin freely in the hole, and you can exert some downward pressure without it slipping off the top of the spindle, it should work.

The spindle should be thicker for the strap drill and bow drill; about the thickness of an adult thumb is a good estimate. One end should be carved to a point, and the other end carved into an arch. The pointy end goes into the bearing block, and the arched end goes onto the baseboard. The baseboard can also be a little thicker—anything up to an inch.

One person will put their foot on the baseboard and exert a downward pressure on the top of the spindle with the bearing block. The other person will wrap the cord around the spindle three or four times and then pull one side of the cord and then the other, keeping a firm pressure between their hands and allowing the friction of the cord to spin the spindle. As before, carve a divot into the baseboard, burn in the hole, and then cut your notch before putting in a big effort for the coal. Place a leaf or a piece of bark under the notch to catch your dust. The longer and smoother the strokes of the cord, the faster you will get a coal.

BOW DRILL

This is the next-most-efficient method of friction fire, after the strap drill. The difference is that it can be done with one person, and your piece of cord needs to be stronger than for the strap drill, as it has more pressure on it through the bow. Your shoelace should still work, but certain types of natural cordage won't be strong enough to withstand the pressure, so you may need to experiment with different types to find one that works.

You will need a slightly bent stick that you tie the cord to each end of. I have seen people that prefer small bows, I have seen people who prefer a bow with a big bend in it, and I have seen people with very long bows. My personal preference is a stick about two feet long that is almost straight. The reason for this is because I can still do nice, long strokes with the bow, but it is manageable and not ungainly. Your bow should be made of a rigid wood, as a flexible wood will lead to your cord slipping on the spindle.

The spindle and baseboard can be prepared as for the strap drill.

The cord needs to be fairly firm between the bow ends, as you want it to grip on to the spindle. Twist the spindle so that the cord is wrapped around it once. If the spindle wants to flip out but can be wrapped, that is a perfect tension. The spindle should be on the outside of the cord, with the arched end on the baseboard and the pointed end in the bearing block.

Place your foot on the baseboard, and anchor the inside of your left forearm to the side of your shin (assuming you are right-handed). This hand will hold the bearing block firmly in place. With your right arm, move the bow in a long, smooth motion back and forth. If you do this slowly at first, you will conserve energy as you build up heat. Once you see lots of smoke from your dust, put in a final big effort.

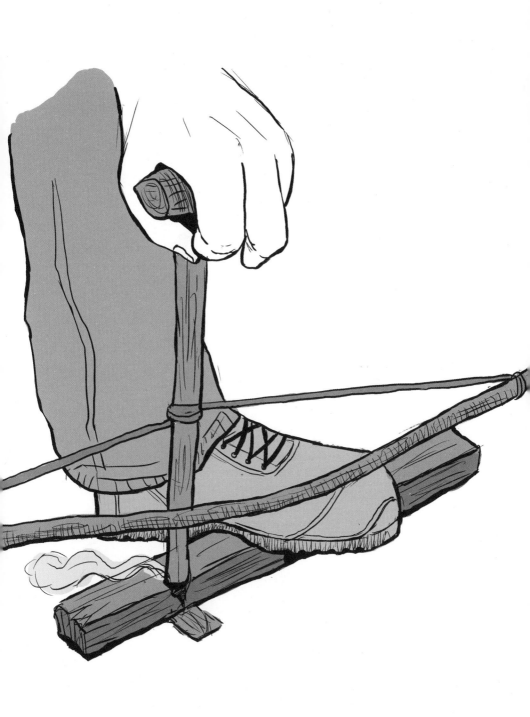

Fire saw

Fire plow

FIRE SAW

Bamboo is the wood of choice for a fire saw, so this will be your go-to if you are lucky enough to find bamboo in your environment. The bamboo must be dead and dry. You will need about a two-foot-long piece, ideally two inches wide. Cut the bamboo in half. Using another piece of bamboo, scrape a handful of dry shavings off of the outside of the bamboo. This will be your tinder bundle. Cut a small notch perpendicular to the sides of the bamboo on the top of one round surface. Place the bamboo facedown with the tinder bundle under this notch. Match the edge of the unscored piece with the notch, press down firmly, and saw back and forth to create friction. If you are successful, the ignited dust will fall onto the tinder bundle, and you will be able to blow it to flame.

FIRE PLOW

Out of all the friction fire methods, I would probably recommend this one last. I have successfully made a fire using this method a few times, but as simple as it looks, it requires a level of angle experimentation that other friction fires lack. It also requires a fair bit of stamina. But if you have no tools and can't make cordage, it is a good one to try. For materials, it just requires a softer wood baseboard and a harder wood "plough," or you can try it with the same wood. The plough is a piece of straight wood with a flattened, sharpened end of about 30 degrees. The baseboard needs a long, straight groove in it and needs to be on a solid surface or able to be anchored down somehow. I find it's best to keep both hands on the plough and your arms straight when ploughing. Moving from the waist and pushing forward on the plough means you will have more stamina to keep going longer. Push the plough back and forth in the groove, creating dust at the far side of the groove. As darker dust forms, speed up and give it your all until the dust pile is smoking on its own.

Good preparation before you begin your fire-making method will enable you to create a sustainable fire to assist in your survival situation.

3.2.3

▶ SUSTAINING FIRE

In a survival situation, it's always best to keep a fire burning constantly. This way you don't have to worry about taking the time to light one every night, and you have a signal ready at any time if a plane flies overhead or a ship passes by your island. You should have a pile of wood that you keep specifically for signaling, so that you're not unprepared if your rescuers come close by. Green boughs work best for creating thick smoke to help attract attention.

In order to sustain a fire without having to constantly attend to it, you will need to set your fire in such a way that it burns slowly but has access to fuel when it needs it.

This largely depends on what type of wood you use, but can also depend on how you set your fire. As mentioned previously, hardwood burns hotter and for longer, and soft wood burns colder and quickly. But there are certain types of wood that hold heat and smolder. Mallee roots in Australia are a good example of this. They will rarely ignite fully but will glow and maintain a coal that you can blow to a flame by adding kindling when you need it. It's good to be observant of the woods you are able to access and use on the fire and what properties they have. Choose the ones that burn hot and bright to bring water to a boil quickly, and the ones that smolder to keep the fire going during the day.

Punk wood, wood that has gotten soft and rotten and then dried out, is fantastic for creating a smoky fire if you want to smoke meats or hides, or keep insects away.

Placing a large hardwood log into a fire will keep it burning for a while, and you can also place logs in a star formation and feed them inward when necessary.

Building a solid crosshatch structure and lighting a small fire on top of that will allow the fire to slowly burn downward through the wood without it burning upward quickly.

If your fire has gone out while you were away from it, try digging down into the ash and coals with some small flammable material handy. Chances are there is enough heat left to ignite your tinder in the hot coals below the surface.

3.2.4

▶ TRANSPORTING FIRE

Many ancient civilizations valued fire so much that it was one person's specific job to take care of it when the tribes traveled from place to place. It is way easier to blow a fire alight from a coal than exert the effort required to start a fire from scratch. Transporting fire was done in a variety of ways, but the theory was the same: allow a coal to have just enough oxygen and fuel that it stays lit, without it being smothered from a lack or burning itself out from consuming it all.

The design was fairly similar to a tinder bundle, with small material around a hot coal wrapped tightly to prevent too much oxygen from getting in. Depending on what you have on hand in your survival scenario, you can use such things as punk wood, charcoal, bracket fungus, dry moss, dry dung (of grass eaters), dry cattail heads, or teased dry grass as the first layer. Then have another layer of thicker material around that, and finish with something to hold it all together tightly. A large animal horn works well, but you can also use some kind of flexible bark tied together with a strip of inner bark.

When traveling with coals, it is a good idea to check on them every now and then to see if they need more fuel or oxygen. It's also a good idea to carry a dry tinder bundle with you, so you can fuel the coal immediately to flame when you get to your next campsite.

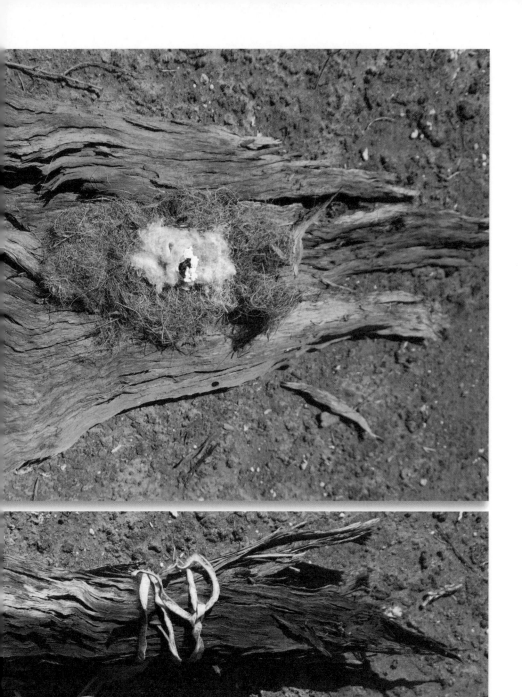

▶ REFLECTIVE FIRES

Usually, the best thing to do in a survival situation is to stay put and wait for rescuers to come to you. If you do have to be on the move, you can use a reflective fire to keep safe and warm at night. This is less labor intensive than a shelter and can be much warmer.

The key is to find a flat wall surface at least three feet high. Lie between this and a low-burning, body-length fire that you've built a wind break on the other side of. This is not a good option if you think it may rain (definitely build or seek shelter if this is the case), and you must also make sure you have enough wood to last the night, as a 3:00 a.m. wood collection run is never a good thing.

A reflector wall can also be built if you have a permanent shelter. Simply build a windbreak on the opposite side of your fire. Although most heat rises, some heat will bounce off the wall and into your shelter, and it will also cut back on the heat that gets pushed away by the wind.

If you choose to locate your fire inside your shelter due to extreme cold or an abundance of biting insects, make sure that your roof is high enough that it doesn't catch fire and that you maintain a low, cooler fire. In the Amazon, I had my fire safely inside my shelter for twenty-one days. The roof of my shelter was four feet high and never even got singed.

AND FINALLY

Some fire rules to remember:

- Clear an area around your fire.

- Don't light a fire you can't control.

- Don't light a fire at the base of a standing tree.

- Always make sure your fire is fully out before permanently leaving an area.

Reflector wall

Reflective fire

3.3

▶ RESCUE

Although the four basic needs of survival are commonly thought of as shelter, water, food, and fire, I include rescue under my basic needs. The reason for this is because the sooner your survival situation ends successfully, the better for you. This will either happen by you figuring out how to get out of the situation, or by someone finding you.

It is recommended in a survival situation to remain where you are when your disaster strikes. If it is a threat to your life to remain in that spot, then move to somewhere your life isn't in immediate danger. Examples of this might be a capsized boat, bushfire, or lack of water.

If your life isn't in immediate danger, staying where you are will present you with your best chance of survival. Not only will you be closer to where rescuers might start to look for you, you won't be potentially moving away from rescuers as they search for you. It also gives you time to create an environment that you could survive in long term if you have to.

I have put myself in challenges where I am moving and trying to survive and where I am staying in one area and trying to survive, and it is always easier to stay put. When you are on the move, you are burning a lot of calories for something other than your immediate survival, and you are lacking the time to ensure that you have adequate shelter, water, and food for the night.

Once you have decided that you need rescuing, and you have taken steps to ensure that shelter, water, and warmth are taken care of, it is time to think about making yourself as visible as possible. How you do this will depend on what resources you have around you and on you. You will need to get inventive. The more visible you can make yourself, the more likely you are to be rescued. Try everything. As silly as it seems, people really have been rescued by putting messages in bottles and floating them out to sea.

3.3.1

▶ SIGNALING

Your rescue is likely to come by means of air, land vehicle, or a rescue mission on foot. You will need to prepare something visible for all these scenarios. Even if you think that you will hear someone who passes by you on foot, you may be sleeping or out collecting water, and they need to know you are around. Generally, you will have about two minutes from the time you hear an aircraft to the time it is out of range, so any signaling needs to be thought out beforehand and ready to go.

Things that will make you more visible to rescuers include:

- Bright colors
- Reflective surfaces
- Straight lines and arrows
- Words on the ground
- Thick smoke
- Bright flames
- Torch trees
- Lights in the dark

BRIGHT COLORS Assuming you have spare gear or clothing with you, hang it from the branches of a high tree, ensuring the leaves don't block the item from view. Place it out in the middle of a clearing, anchored so it doesn't blow away. Use branches or rocks to make an arrow to indicate the location of your shelter. Use bright green vegetation on darker surfaces to write a message for aerial search parties. Building a tepee structure to hang your bright and colorful pieces from is also a good idea, as the tepee structure itself will draw the eye.

REFLECTIVE SURFACES While a signal mirror is ideal, assuming you don't have one on you, any reflective surface will do. Utilize garbage that you might find around you, such as polished cans or glass bottles. These will catch the sun's rays, causing a flash of bright light observable from up to two miles away. Hang these in trees around your location. When the wind blows, they will move and signal without you needing to tend to them. Have a polished surface on you at all times in case you hear a vehicle. The front of a mobile phone will work even if you are out of signal or your battery has died. Practice reflecting the sun's rays until you know how to aim them.

AERIAL RESCUE hold your hand to the sky where the plane is and direct the light from the sun to your hand; remove your hand, and you know that the light should be visible from the plane.

GROUND RESCUE reflect the light to the ground, and then direct it in a straight line to the vehicle or person.

Keep signaling until you know that you have been seen. You will know this when you receive some kind of acknowledgment from the rescue party. It may be in the form of a signal back, a change of course, or a low flyover of the aircraft.

Straight lines and arrows Nature rarely constructs in straight lines, so any structure with straight lines stands out; lines and arrows made of rocks, branches, or leaves pointing to your location or the direction you are traveling will all attract attention.

Words on the ground SOS was accepted as the worldwide signal for distress in 1906. Although many people believe it is an acronym for something, it was chosen because it translates easily in Morse code (three dots, three dashes, three dots). HELP would also work, but would require knowledge of the English language. If you are writing words on the ground, make sure you do them in a cleared area, easily visible from above. Make them as large as you can, and try to distinguish them in some way from the ground you are creating them on. Straight-line letters work best, as they don't blend in with nature as easily. Make sure you destroy your words when you are rescued, to ensure people don't think someone still needs saving.

Thick smoke During the day, thick white or black smoke will get attention. If you have managed to get a fire started for your camp, make sure that you keep it burning all day, every day. Have separate fires set up for signal fires, with dry, extremely flammable fuel ready to go. These fires should be out in the open and large. Fires under trees will be hard to see and may start a forest fire if they get out of control. It's best if you can prepare more than one fire area with three fires, which is a universally accepted number for a distress signal. Green leaves will burn with a thick white smoke, and anything rubber will burn with a thick black smoke.

WHEN THE GRID FAILS

Bright flames At night it's best to have a fire that burns brightly rather than produces smoke. Dry wood and dead leaves will flare up brightly in the dark to shine a light on your location.

Torch trees Build a fire in a tree by filling the lower limbs with flammable kindling. When you light the lower branches, the whole tree will catch on fire, sending out a signal that will last for longer than your average fire. Just make sure you choose a tree that is separate from the forest, so you don't cause a wildfire.

Lights in the dark If you do have a flashlight with you, save the battery for when you truly need it. Signaling for help is going to be way more useful than having it on for comfort during the night. Your phone screen lights up, and most phones today have a flashlight function, so save your battery if you don't have service. Amplify these lights at night by shining them off something reflective, such as tin cans or shiny surfaces. Three short flashes followed by three long flashes and three short flashes will indicate your distress to anyone in the area. Pause for a minute and signal again.

We have all seen the movies where the hero runs to signal the rescue ship or plane as it moves past their location, only to be too late and for rescue to pass them by. As focused as you need to be on your basic needs, your overall aim is to get out of there, so spend the time in the early days of your scenario to be prepared to make the most of any sign of possible help.

3.3.2

▶ NAVIGATION

If you have decided that a rescue is not coming or that to stay in an area is risking your life, you will need to leave your initial location. Make a plan about the direction you want to head in, based on your best chance of being rescued or making it to civilization. If you had familiarized yourself with your area prior to your emergency, you may have an exact or rough idea of which direction to travel. If you are unsure, heading to a high point to check out the surrounding terrain is a good idea. Try to locate signs of civilization, such as fences, windmills, and rail tracks. Follow your best hope for survival if you are unsure of where to start. In a desert, this will mean following water signs, and in a swamp, this may mean heading inland or toward signs of dry land.

If you are on foot, you will need a system to ensure you walk in a straight line. Humans have a natural tendency to walk veering to the left or right if they don't have a point to walk toward. This means that you will end up wasting a lot of energy walking in circles. Scientists have a lot of theories behind this, but no answer yet. If you don't have a compass and are trying to walk in a set direction, there are a few ways of achieving this. The first is to sight something in the distance in the direction you want to go and walk to that. Once you get to that object, place it at your back and find another object to aim for. This will work in relatively clear terrain but isn't so effective in heavily wooded areas. Another method is using catchment features and "aiming off." This means that you sight a feature you are trying to head toward that has an obvious feature that funnels toward it. This may be a valley pass with a river in front or a farmer's water tank along a fence line. Purposely head to one side of the landmark so that when you are "caught" by the feature, you know that you have to head in a certain direction to get to the landmark.

If you know which direction you want to head in but are unsure how to find that direction or how to stay walking in that direction, there are some good clues in nature.

DAY NAVIGATION

At its very simplest, the sun rises in the east and sets in the west. It then gets a little more complicated, as the rest depends on whether you are located in the Southern or Northern Hemisphere. At the equator, the sun's path will draw a perfect line in the sky overhead. The farther away you go from the equator, the less overhead the sun will be and the more south or north tending it will be, depending on the season or time of year.

In the Southern Hemisphere, the sun follows a path that tends southerly in winter and northerly in summer; in the Northern Hemisphere, the sun follows a path that tends northerly in winter and southerly in the summer. This means that walking with the sun on your back or at your shoulder will only give you a very rough idea of a direction to walk in, and you will need to be aware of when the sun has hit its peak and begins heading down, to prevent you from getting turned around.

To make a basic compass, stand in the sun as it rises and draw a line that runs parallel to your shadow. That is east–west. Put an E at the side closest to you and a W to the side farthest from you. Draw a perpendicular bisecting line, and label the end of the one to your right with an N and the end of the one to your left with an S. You now have a compass. Sight a landmark in the direction you wish to head in, based on this compass, and walk there.

If you don't know what time of day it is or want to recheck the bearing that you are walking on, you will need to set up a sundial.

SUNDIAL This requires a straight stick and two rocks. Plant the stick upright in the ground, and place a stone at the tip of the shadow. As the sun moves, so will the shadow. Wait at least half an hour, and place a second rock at the tip of the shadow. Mark a line between the two rocks, and lay a stick to perpendicularly bisect it. This will be your compass. Stand with your back to the upright stick and your feet on either side of the stick on the ground, and you will be facing a northerly direction.

Many stars are different in the Northern and Southern Hemispheres. Most stars move through the sky at night, changing position and visibility quite rapidly. This means you shouldn't pick just any star in the sky and follow it for the night.

In the Northern Hemisphere, the only visible star in the night sky that remains in the same spot is Polaris, or the North Star. This is because it is in the center of the star field, and Earth's axis points almost directly toward it. It may be difficult to locate the North Star because it isn't the brightest star in the night sky, but the Big Dipper and Cassiopeia are two very obvious constellations nearby that can help guide you to Polaris.

Polaris is not visible in the Southern Hemisphere, and there are no stars that remain constant. To find south, you will need to locate the Southern Cross and its two Pointer stars. Draw a line between the two long points of the cross, and then create a line that does a perpendicular bisection of a line between the two pointers. Where these two lines meet in the sky, draw a line down to the horizon, and that will always be south.

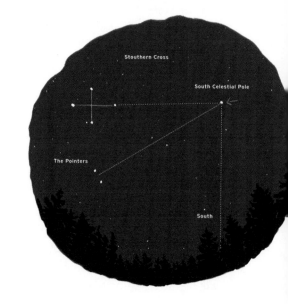

Again, these natural indicators will change sides of the compass, depending on which hemisphere you are in, but if you know that they will always be on a specific side, it might save you from walking in circles.

Moss likes cooler, damper environments, so it tends to grow on the side of the tree that gets less sun. Termite mounds tend to be on the side that gets more sun. Snow and ice will thaw faster on the sunny side of rocks, and the prevailing winds will shape the trees in the area, helping you to head on a bearing. Use as many natural clues as you can to piece together which direction to head in, because there are always exceptions to these rules that can get you turned around.

If you are by a river, follow it downstream. Bigger rivers tend to have villages or towns on their banks, and where they empty into the ocean, there may be ports and cities.

To decide how much daylight you have left, hold up three fingers to the sun-side horizon. Each three fingers that the sun is above the horizon signals an hour of time. Always make sure that you set up a shelter and establish fire before it gets dark when you are traveling.

Hopefully you came prepared with a GPS, compass, and map of the area and familiarized yourself with your surroundings. If you didn't, utilizing any or all of the above navigational aids may help you make your way to safety and quickly end your survival scenario.

3.4

▶ SHELTER

Exposure can kill you faster than dehydration or starvation. You can last up to three days without water, but one night in cold temperatures can be the end of you. The night temperature does not need to drop below freezing to be deadly. Even a seemingly warm night with a little bit of rain and a fresh breeze can potentially lead to hypothermia. My worst bouts of hypothermia were in the tropical Amazon jungle on a windy, rainy night where the air temperature didn't drop below 59°F.

A shelter will also prevent excess exposure to heat by providing relief from the sweltering sun.

Besides giving protection from the elements, a shelter provides a refuge, a place to gather your thoughts and to plan your next move. Having a roof over your head is going to make you feel a lot better about your situation.

Because of this, I highly recommend that if you can't get a fire going on the first day of your survival situation, you make sure that you have a shelter constructed before it gets dark.

194

Your body loses its heat to the environment in five different ways:

1. RESPIRATION

This happens when your body inhales cold air and works to warm it by heating that air before breathing it out. This results in a loss of body heat via your breath.

2. RADIATION

This happens when your body temperature is higher than your environment's and your body heat will exit your exposed skin to warm your environment. Your head, neck, wrists, and ankles contribute up to 60 percent of a loss of body heat, due to their increased blood flow compared to other areas of the body, so it's important to try to keep them covered.

3. EVAPORATION

This happens when the skin has expelled moisture, such as sweat, and this evaporates, causing a cooling of the skin's surface. This usually happens in hot climates, but working up a sweat in a cold climate can result in hypothermia if the skin is not covered up and dried off quickly.

4. CONVECTION

This happens with heat loss by air or water moving across the skin's surface. This includes exposure to one or more of the following: cold air, rain, and wind.

5. CONDUCTION

This happens when heat loss occurs by direct contact with an object. Heat exits the warmer object to equalize the temperatures between the two objects. This can occur when sitting or lying on cold ground or up against cold rocks.

A good shelter will take into consideration as many of these methods of heat loss as possible and work to combat them.

3.4.1

▶ CHOOSING YOUR SHELTER LOCATION

In survival, calories are your greatest asset. Maintaining them is the difference between life and death, so it is imperative to use as few of them as possible. One way people tend to waste calories is by rushing into building their shelter and making the wrong type in the wrong area. This leads to having to construct another one at some stage. Taking the time to explore your options before building is essential. Locations, priorities, and materials all vary, but there are some hard rules I stick to when choosing my location.

Apart from trying to ensure that where you lie is going to be flat, make sure that the shelter:

- Isn't on or close to any insect nests or pathways.

- Isn't on or close to animal pathways or homes.

- Isn't below any tidal or flood marks.

- Isn't located on dry creek beds; even if you can't see any rain, distant rain can still cause flooding from hundreds of miles away.

- Isn't under any dead or heavy-looking tree branches.

- Has the door or entrance facing away from prevailing winds.

As a general rule, if you are on high, exposed ground, try to get down lower to a less exposed location, and, conversely, if you are on low, wet ground, try to get to higher ground. Also look for an area that has good access to water without being so close that you will suffer from the insects that usually also inhabit those areas.

Shelter location rules at a glance:

Avoid insect nests
or pathways.

Avoid animal pathways
or homes.

Avoid areas below tidal
or flood marks.

Avoid dry
creek beds.

Avoid dead or heavy-
looking tree branches.

Face entrance away from
prevailing winds.

3.4.2

▶ MAKING YOUR ENVIRONMENT WORK FOR YOU

The less effort something takes for you to do, the longer you will survive in an emergency scenario. This doesn't mean being lazy with what you do, because a badly built shelter isn't really a shelter at all. This simply means that wherever you can, let nature do your job. In most environments, you will find a partially ready emergency shelter already created for you. Remember that you need to get out of the wind and rain and off the ground for a shelter to help save your life.

Some things to look out for that will make building a shelter easier:

A. **Fallen trees**
B. **Hollow logs**
C. **Root systems**
D. **Caves and overhangs**
E. **Natural hollows**
F. **Stone barriers**
G. **Snow trenches**

These types of natural occurrences can be made into a cozy home with little effort from you. You end up closing gaps and adding material to the roof, sides, and floor rather, than building an entire shelter from scratch.

You will need to ensure that a couple things are okay before inhabiting your already created shelter:

1. **Make sure that it doesn't already have locals.** This includes checking caves for recent animal signs and making sure any insects and spiders that share the space are friendly.

2. **Make sure that it has sufficient air flow and ventilation.** Although we are trying to prevent wind from moving through the shelter, carbon dioxide poisoning can occur if you don't allow some oxygen to circulate.

3.4.3

▶ PROPERTIES OF A GOOD SHELTER

Creating a bad shelter is almost worse than creating no shelter at all. There is something demoralizing about making an effort to build something to protect you from the environment if it lets in the wind and rain, and you shiver through the night. A shelter will probably require daily maintenance to ensure it retains these properties, but it's easier to do five minutes of upkeep a day than to rebuild from scratch over and over.

In the Amazon, the palm leaves I used to keep my shelter waterproof in monsoon storms would wilt within days, and if I didn't put twenty fresh palms on each day, the rain would pour in. I made this maintenance part of my morning routine. It didn't take much time at all, yet ensured the integrity of my shelter.

The properties of a good shelter are as follows:

1. **Flat area to lie on:** Sleep is a very important part of your mental well-being, so the better you can make your bedding area, the better sleep you will have.

2. **Sized to fit all required occupants:** Quite often people get carried away with making large shelters, but remembering that physical work requires calories to complete, you are best off building a small shelter; it will also be easier to warm the space if it is smaller.

3. **No other inhabitants:** One way to ensure this is to clear the ground beneath your whole shelter; insects love leaf litter and will tend to be more prolific if you haven't cleared the ground.

4. **Structural integrity:** Make sure that the frame is solid and strong; you will be piling layers of sticks, leaves, and other thatching material onto that frame, and you don't want it collapsing midbuild or when you are asleep underneath it.

5. **Windproof:** Ensure that all openings are facing away from prevailing winds and, where possible, protected from the elements; build your shelter in a way that the materials you use for the walls and roof don't blow away in a storm and are thick enough to prevent most of the wind from moving through your shelter.

6. **Waterproof:** You will need far more materials than you think to keep the rain from coming in when it is stormy out. A good rule of thumb is that if you can see sunlight coming in through the shelter's roof in the daytime, the rain will get in. See thatching methods (page 70) to learn good tips on waterproofing.

▶ DIFFERENT TYPES OF SHELTERS

There are many different types of survival shelters. If it can protect you from the chill of the earth and the elements of the sky, it can be called a survival shelter. The first form of shelter is the clothes on your back, so if you have nothing else and no time to make something, try to cover your wrists, ankles, head, and neck and sit with your back to the wind if you are in an exposed position. Anything more than this is a bonus. Keeping in mind the ways your body loses heat to the environment, pile up some leaves or grasses to get off the ground and stuff some in your shirt and pants (making sure that it is not poisonous, prickly, or occupied). This will store heat in pockets like a makeshift down jacket and prevent all your heat from escaping. The following pages feature increasingly advanced types of shelters.

The Leaf Box, see page 206

The Lean-To, see page 208

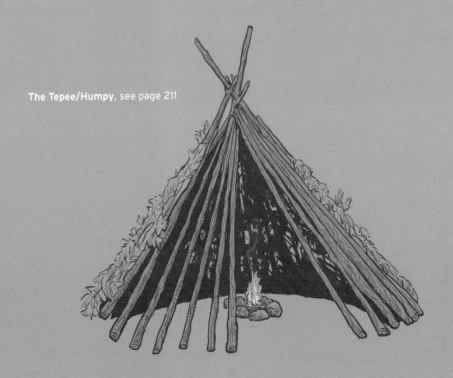

The Tepee/Humpy, see page 211

THE LEAF BOX

This is the simplest construction for a shelter and is a good one to know for emergencies. If it was late in the day and I suddenly found myself in need of a shelter to get through the night, I would use this one.

It is quick to assemble, but it is not usually that comfortable or waterproof, so don't use this construction in a long-term survival scenario. However, it will enable you to last through a night out in the wilderness. Its primary function is to get you off the ground and protect you from the wind.

The leaf box requires about eight body-length and six body-width pieces of wood. They are laid down in a crosshatch box form. Alternatively, you can do this in a ready-made hollow or ditch.

You will then need to fill the box with as much leaf litter and grass as possible, remembering that when you lie on the leaves and branches, they will squash quite flat. The idea is that you will crawl into the middle of the leaves, so you will need enough to insulate the ground and also to completely cover you to protect you from the elements. If done properly, this has the potential to keep you dry in a rain shower and warm in freezing temperatures.

One thing to be careful of is what types of critters you invite into your leaf box for the night. Some piles of leaf litter may house an ant nest, scorpions, spiders, or other creatures that will make for an uncomfortable night's sleep. Remember, at the end of the day, we are looking at survival, not comfort, so the more foliage you can pile into your box, the better.

THE LEAN-TO

A lean-to is a little more labor intensive than a leaf box, but if done properly, it is more waterproof and windproof and better for a long-term survival
scenario. Although it seems very open sided, you can fill in the ends of the
lean-to to add further protection from the wind and rain. I usually position
my fire along the open edge of the lean-to, which allows me to access
a full-body warmth that bounces off the back of the lean-to and adds a
reflective heat.

To conserve energy, look for a place where the frame has partly constructed itself. Examples of this include a fallen tree or a hollowed-out tree trunk.
Anywhere one windproof wall is already built will cut down on the labor required. One thing to note is that rock faces do not usually make good walls,
as they generally get very cold at night and suck the warmth away from
your body, rather than helping to keep you warm.

If you are unable to find a suitable natural portion for your shelter, you will
need to find two supports, such as stumps or suitably placed crooks of a
tree branch, to rest the main beam on. Make sure the main beam is long
enough so you can lie down completely underneath. Then use sticks to
make struts on one side of the main branch, securing them with string or
grasses where possible. Cover these sticks with whatever thatching material is available to you. This could be leaves, grasses, moss, bark, or even clay
and mud. The important thing to keep in mind is that you want it to be able
to withstand wind and rain.

This is also the best shelter to build
for shade in extreme heat, as it will
allow some wind flow as well as keep
you out of the sun.

THE TEPEE/HUMPY

This shelter is the most labor intensive, but it is the one I would build if I found myself in a long-term survival scenario in a colder climate.

When built properly, it is waterproof and tall enough to sit in, and it gives you the option to have a fire inside that will keep you snug through a very cold night.

There are many ways of building tepees, but the best way I know is to find three long branches (around six feet long works well) that each have a fork in the end. Prop the sticks into the ground and intertwine the forks so that each of the three sticks is holding up the others, resulting in a structure that stand strong on its own. Place them wide enough apart that you can lie down within the circle they make, and ensure that they are tall enough that you can sit underneath them comfortably.

The next step is to find other sticks and fill in the gaps between your three main sticks. Then cover with branches, leaves, and other natural materials, placing them over the frame you've made. Keep going until you can sit inside and not see any daylight through the walls. Make sure that you leave a hole to crawl in and out of.

The trick with having a fire in the structure is allowing for a breathing hole in the roof of the tepee for the smoke to escape. If you are in a rainy location, you can waterproof this hole by making a cover from intertwined branches and leaves and placing it over the protruding ends of your frame, so it rests above the hole.

In a space as small as a tepee, you will only require a tiny twig fire to warm the space during the night. Locate the fire at the center of the tepee and keep it small, or else you may end up burning down your shelter, destroying all your hard work.

A humpy, or wurly, is the Australian Indigenous form of a tepee and tends to be similar in design, but with a more rounded rooftop. I would choose to make a whirly over a tepee if I was unable to find long, solid struts for the three main supporting beams.

THE A-FRAME

I can almost hear every survivalist screaming at me: "But what about the A-frame?" This shelter tends to be at the top of most survival shelter lists, but there is a good reason that I don't recommend it in my top three. In fact, I wouldn't even mention it at all except for the fact it is such a popular design, and I feel like I need to warn people away from it being their go-to. I was one of those people who thought it was the best design to build, but then on two occasions it almost resulted in my death from hypothermia, so this advice is coming from very personal experiences.

I think that the fact it looks like a tent or a house is a comfort to people, and because it has walls on more sides, there is the added psychological aspect of feeling safer.

With the A-frame, unless you have some form of man-made material like a poncho or a tarp, the roof is very hard to make waterproof at its peak. It's not impossible, and there are a few methods of weaving and thatching with an additional building piece that can help, but it is an added complication. In addition, due to its shape, it is very hard to warm the space, as a fire needs to be at one end, and this results in either very cold feet or a very cold head. By the time the heat has circulated enough to warm the space, it has leaked out through the natural roof.

I believe that when we are looking at survival skills, we need to be looking at the ancient skills our ancestors used thousands of years ago. There are very few, if any, examples of A-frame shelters in primitive societies. The lean-to, tepee, and humpy were the most common designs for a reason, and my own experiences have proven why.

3.4.5

▶ NATURAL CORDAGE

This is one of those areas where bush-craft and survival share some crossover. There are books written solely about the art of making rope and cord using natural materials, and if it interests you, there are courses about it that would be a valuable addition to your personal tool kit of skills. Rope can be invaluable for many things, including building shelters, making traps and snares, and making shoes to protect your feet. I'm only going to touch on the basics of making natural cordage, as you won't die if you don't know this, but it can come in handy, especially with making a solid shelter.

Leaves for cordage

Just about any strong, flexible fiber can be used as cordage. This includes:

- Leaves
- Roots
- Stems
- Vines
- Outer bark
- Inner bark
- Grasses
- Hair
- Wool
- Animal intestines
- Animal sinew
- Animal skin

Cordage from leaves

Outer bark for cordage

Animal intestine cord

Inner bark for cordage

Cord from animal skin

Cordage from wool

Animal sinew cord

Certain types of each of these things are better for making cord than others. Your best bet is to experiment with the resources around you. Grab some grasses, and try to tie a piece around something. If it holds, it works. If it doesn't, try something else.

LEAVES Although any long, thin leaf can be utilized as cord if it is strong enough, the best leaves for cord are from plants such as aloes and yuccas that have juicy, fibrous leaves. By placing the leaf on a flat surface and scraping the juicy flesh away with a flat edge, you are left with bundles of thin fibers that can be plaited together to create strong rope.

ROOTS If you are in a swamp or wetland area, you may be able to reach under the water and into the mud to access root systems. Some roots are too brittle to use, but water-soaked ones work perfectly.

STEMS Ideal plants to use will have long, string-like fibers when you split them. You can use some stems when they are green, but most of these types of plants work best when they are dry.

VINES The woodier a vine is, the less likely it is to be good for cord. Look for a flexible vine that you can tie in a knot without it snapping. Vines work best when fresh. The drier a vine is, the more brittle it becomes.

OUTER BARK Outer bark works best when fresh. A way to find suitable outer bark is to bend a twig on the tree. When the stick breaks, check to see if the outer layer of bark is still attached on one side. Pull the inner bits apart, and see if the bark easily peels away from the inner branch. If it does, then it should make good rope. Just make sure you don't harvest bark from around the whole tree, because it will kill the tree. Instead, just remove it in patches or from branches.

INNER BARK Inner bark is best harvested and processed from dry wood. If you break a branch apart and you can peel the bark from the inner wood in long strips, then it will be good for rope. Simply peel the inner layer off the bark you have removed. It will be in long fibers and perfect to be used as is or to be reverse wrapped for extra durability.

GRASSES These include most kinds of rushes, such as bullrush and cattail. They are best used when green. If possible, try to harvest the longest leaves and cut at the base rather than pull out at the roots, so as not to destroy the resource.

HAIR/WOOL Look for the carcasses of hairy or wooly animals, or use the fur or wool from those that you hunt for food. Nothing needs to go to waste out there.

ANIMAL SKIN Again, it's best used if wet or processed to leather. Cut it into strips, and reverse wrap for a good, solid rope.

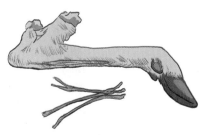 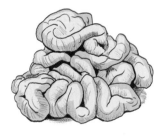

ANIMAL SINEW It's best to use sinew when it's wet. This means it doesn't need processing, and you can use it straight out of the animal. If it has dried out, then a bit of water will bring it back to a usable state. Our ancestors used to pop it in their mouth and chew it before they used it, when they didn't have an excess of water available. The good thing about sinew is that it shrinks as it dries, so it cinches even tighter, creating a good bond.

ANIMAL INTESTINES I have experimented with smaller animals and have personally found that with any animal smaller than a pig, the intestines are too weak to work well as rope. I have heard of people using smaller animals, but I have not seen it myself. The intestines require cleaning, drying, and salting to be used as rope, but if you happen to be by an ocean or salt lake, then you are in luck and can create solid rope. The intestines work best if you use the reverse wrap to create your rope (see page 221).

I don't tend to process the fibers I use for rope with shelter building; I use it in its purest form. This is because processing enough plant fibers for the amount of cordage required to tie together all beams and joins of a shelter takes a lot of time, and shelter is a priority that needs to be taken care of quickly in a survival situation. It is also possible to build a good shelter without using any rope, so if materials are scarce, don't get hung up on the need for it; just use friction and balance to make your shelter strong.

ADDING STRENGTH TO YOUR FIBERS

A simple way of remembering how to strengthen fibers is to recall that two is better than one. If I have one cord and it is breaking, by adding another strand of fiber, I am making it stronger. At a very basic level, if you have one leaf and it is breaking as you try to tie your shelter up, add another leaf to the bundle and see if it holds. Twisting the two together also adds another level of strength.

Plaiting or reverse wrapping will make your rope or cord more durable and reusable. It takes some time and resources to do, but in a long-term survival situation, rope can assist in making things to make your time out there more comfortable. The only time you should focus on making cordage first in a survival situation is making a short piece of cordage for a bow drill, if you need to get a fire going and this method is your best option.

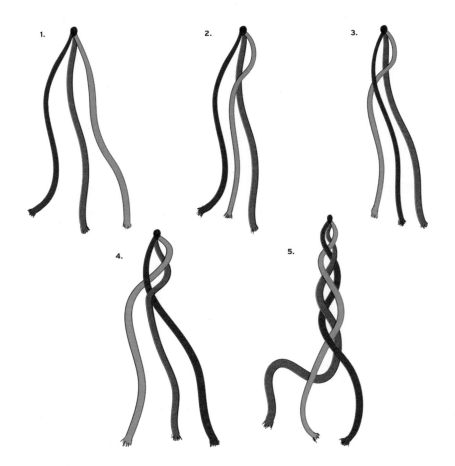

PLAITING

The reason I recommend this as one way of making rope is that it is a technique that most of us have used at some stage in our lives, so it isn't a new skill to learn. It does the job of adding strength to fibers, and its only disadvantage is that it results in a flat rope that doesn't slide over itself nicely. This means it isn't great to use with traps and snares. As I'm all for keeping survival as simple as possible, if you can only remember how to plait, then do that to strengthen your rope.

For those who have never done a plait before, or if it has been a while, you need three strands of fiber. Tie a knot with them all at the top, and then take the outside right strand and feed it over the middle strand. Then take the outside left strand and feed it over the middle strand. Repeat until you have the length of rope you require, and tie a knot on the end.

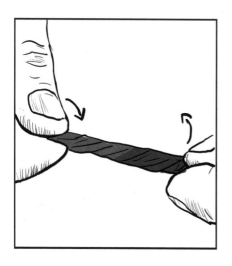

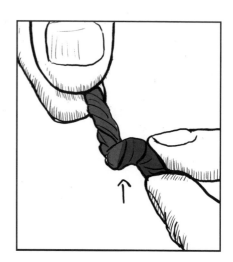

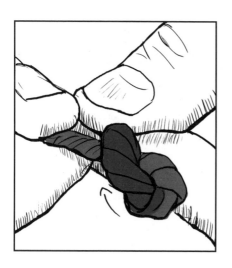

THE REVERSE WRAP

Take a length of fibers in both hands. Start with your hands a few inches apart, and twist your hands in opposite directions until a loop forms in the fibers. Usually, I then place that loop in my mouth, but you can also pinch it between your thumb and forefinger. If you are holding it in your mouth, hold the two lengths of fibers so you have one in each hand. Twist the lengths both in the same direction until the fibers tighten, and then wrap the two lengths around each other in the opposite direction.

If you are twisting and wrapping in the same direction, your rope will unravel when you let it go. If you are twisting and wrapping in the opposite direction, the rope will pinch into itself, and this is what you want. Keep doing this until your rope is at your required length.

One thing to remember about natural fibers is that they tend to be shorter than the length of rope you require, so rather than end your rope when the fibers run out, you can splice in more fibers.

Splicing Natural Fibers

Splicing simply involves adding lengths of fiber to existing threads when they begin to get too short to wrap. It is best to add new fibers in when the existing threads are between an inch and an inch and a half long. You place the new fibers along the length of the existing fibers and continue to wrap, incorporating the new fibers in with the old. Another tip is to only add one length of thread in at a time and allow for a couple of inches of wrap before adding another length in; otherwise you will end up with a weak spot in your rope.

3.4.6

▶ KNOTS

Knots are another area where bushcraft and survival overlap in such a way that I feel obligated to make the distinction. Do you need a knowledge of knots in order to survive? Absolutely not. Will it help you survive? Maybe. I firmly believe that if you know how to tie your shoelaces, then you know enough knots to survive. We've all heard the saying "if you don't know knots, then tie lots," and that sums it up for me. I have survived for over a hundred days in various locations around the world with no resources and never tied anything more complex than a reef knot—right over left and then left over right. In fact, most natural fibers won't take a complex knot in their pure form, so that knowledge wouldn't help at all. But, as I have also stated, the more knowledge in your personal tool kit, the better, so I am going to cover what I consider to be the more useful knots for a survival situation.

THE OVERHAND KNOT

It is the simplest of all knots, but the most useful in a survival situation for tying off the top of fibers if you are making cordage. Make a loop and pass the end through.

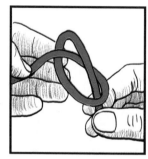

THE REEF KNOT

This is a very secure knot that is easily untied. When tying a reef knot, tie right over left, and then, instead of going right over left again, you go left over right. This knot is useful for tying the ends of rope or cordage together.

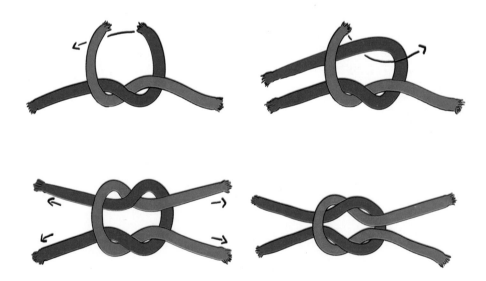

TRUCKER'S HITCH

This knot is great for cinching something tight. Tie a loop in one end of a rope (any way you like), and then feed the other end of the rope through the loop and pull down hard, tying this loose end off with a couple of half hitches.

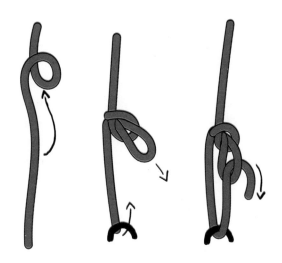

HALF HITCH

The half hitch is a valuable knot to finish off the ends of other knots, to assist in making them secure. It's a simple overhand knot where the working end of a line is brought over and under the standing part.

Knots don't need to be fancy, and you don't have to know their names—they just need to work. If something needs to be made secure, no one will be judging you on your knot tying when they rescue you. Do whatever you can to make things safe and secure.

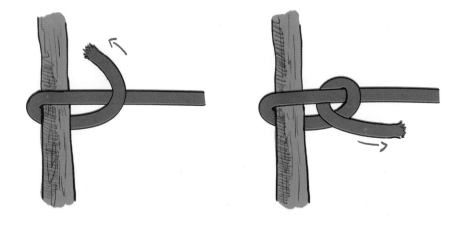

3.4.7

▶ LASHING

Another skill that will assist with making a strong and secure shelter is the art of lashing. Lashing is the technique of winding rope in such a way that it secures two or more items together. There are many different lashing techniques, but the most important one for shelter building is square lashing. This is for lashing two branches or beams that cross.

Secure one end of the cord to one of the branches; then weave the line alternatively above and below both branches in a complete clockwise circuit. Make a loop around one of the branches before weaving the rope over and under the branches in a counterclockwise direction. Do this a few times before tying off the end of the rope with two half hitches. The more firmly you can do the looping, the more secure the lashing will be.

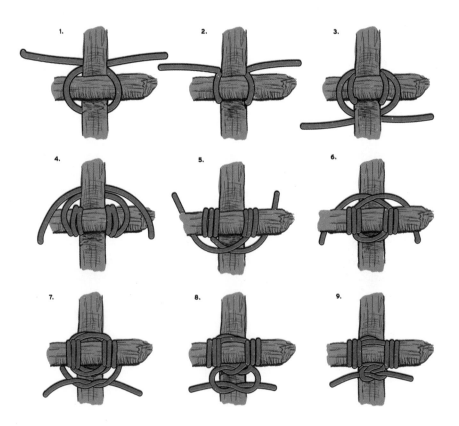

▶ THATCHING

There are many different types of thatching used to make the roof of a primitive structure waterproof. I stick with the most basic method for my shelters, and that is to always start from the bottom and work upward, like the tiles of a roof. This will ensure that the overlapping layers push water to the outside of the shelter, rather than funneling it into the shelter.

3.4.9

▶ SHELTER TIPS

Once your shelter is built, it is important to make sure it functions well for you in your survival situation, so here are a few final shelter tips:

Keep your shelter organized If your shelter is a mess, then it's hard to find the things you need. This may not seem like a big deal during the day, but if your fire goes out at night and you can't find more wood, being able to lay your hands on your flashlight or tinder in the dark could save your life.

Don't eat or prepare food in your shelter Your shelter needs to be a safe and comfortable place for you to sleep. Predators are usually drawn into a camp by food smells, so choose an area fifty to a hundred yards from where you sleep to make your kitchen area. Even if you don't attract the larger animals into the area, uncomfortable nuisances like ants and mice can also be drawn in by food smells, so keep your shelter as clean as possible.

Have your toilet area away from your shelter For sanitary reasons, and a level of your comfort, choose an area away from camp to make your toilet area. My only exception to this is in areas where creating a circle of urine around your camp may assist in deterring predators. But even then, make it a large circle.

Make sure you keep the things you need dry inside the shelter Seems like common sense, but sometimes I have left fire-starting tinder or items of clothing outside my shelter if it doesn't look stormy, only for a storm to soak everything. I always make sure I store a little stash of dry fire-making materials in my shelter for emergencies.

Realize you are effectively camouflaged from rescue You have made a solid shelter entirely out of natural materials. Nothing about that shelter will stand out to people searching for you, and they may pass right by you in a ground search if you happen to be sleeping. Find some way to make your location stand out to the people looking for you.

4.5

▶ FOOD

Out of all your survival needs, food might be the most confusing one to come to terms with. There is a comfort to having three solid meals a day, and we are taught that to have any less is to be "starving." Food is the one need that you can last the longest without. On average, people can last up to three weeks without food. This will depend on your body type and how many calories you are burning in a day, but it does give you plenty of time to take care of your other needs before worrying about filling your stomach. I find that I am most effective without food on days one and two, and then again on days five to twelve in an extreme survival scenario. Days three and four seem to fall under detoxing and getting used to a new normal. No matter how healthy our diet is prior to an extreme survival scenario, our bodies are used to all sorts of chemical additives that can cause fatigue, headaches, and nausea when we are deprived of them.

A healthy body can survive for some time on the reserves in its tissues, but a lack of food eventually makes it increasingly difficult to make good decisions, keep warm, recover from hard work, and fight off infections.

The bad news is that food can be quite an elusive thing in a survival scenario, if you don't know what you are looking for or how to get it. There are millions of different plants and animals throughout the world, so I am going to make things as simple as I can to help you make good eating choices in your location.

There are two different types of food groups in the wild: flora (plants) and fauna (animals). While plants may be easier to gather since they don't run away, animals provide far more energy when consumed. It becomes a calories-in-versus-calories-out equation that you need to assess for yourself. If you can trap or hunt animals without burning too many calories, then the reward in energy is worth the effort. If you will burn an excess of calories chasing down your prey, then it may be best to gather wild edible plants instead. What best suits your situation?

3.5.1

▶ PLANTS

As always, there are exceptions to every rule of thumb in survival, so if you are 100 percent certain of your plant identification and you know something is edible even if it goes against the advice of my general rules of what not to eat, eat it. **If you can't positively identify it as something you can eat, don't eat it until you have worked through my toxin testing steps, especially if it has any of the characteristics of the items on my list of what to avoid.**

▶ WHAT TO AVOID

Time and time again, people will hold up examples of edible, nutritious plants that have some of the following characteristics. I understand and agree that there are plants that won't kill you that fit these rules. However, most of the time plants that are on the list have the potential to make you sick or hasten your death. Since we all must start somewhere in a disaster scenario, I recommend you avoid consuming all plants that you can't identify that fit in these categories:

Beans, bulbs, seed pods:
Rosary Peas

- Mushrooms or fungi

- Milky or discolored sap

- Beans, bulbs, or seeds inside pods

- Spines, fine hairs, or thorns

- An almond or peachy scent

- Grains with pink, purple, or black spikes on them

- Red plants

- Fruit that divides into five segments

- Three-leaf growth patterns, i.e., three leaves on the same twig stem

- Trumpet- or bell-shaped flowers

- Stems with leaves on opposite sides

Mushrooms or fungi:
Death Cap Mushroom

The next move to finding out what is edible in the plant kingdom around you is to experiment. The important thing about experimenting with eating plants is that you take your time and **do all the toxin testing steps.**

Three leaves:
Poison Ivy

Five-segment fruit:
Jamaican Ackee

Trumpet-shaped flowers:
Angel's Trumpet

Leaves on opposite sides:
Poison Sumac

3.5.1.2

▶ TESTING FOR TOXINS

There is a myth that if an animal is eating a certain plant, then we can eat that plant. This is false information and could get you killed. Animals have very different digestive tracts to ours, and some have evolved to remove certain toxins from plants to survive eating them. The animal that has the closest digestive system to our own is the monkey, and even then, monkeys can consume certain things we can't. I personally have survived in the jungle eating the fruits I have observed monkeys eating. They will even be so good as to throw some at you or drop it to the ground to save you the trouble of climbing the tree yourself. I always put that fruit through my test for toxins before eating.

THE TOXIN TEST

1. **Inspect:** Make sure it doesn't look rotten or moldy; remove any insects or insect casings.

2. **Smell:** You are looking for an almond or peachy smell; if it smells like marzipan or peach, discard immediately.

3. **Skin irritation:** Wipe the plant on the inside of your wrist, which is delicate and more likely to react to an irritant; if your skin gets red or swollen, or develops a rash, discard the plant.

4. **Lips:** Wipe the plant on the inside of your lip; if irritation occurs, wash the area thoroughly and discard the plant.

5. **Swallow:** Take a small piece of the plant, consume it, and do not eat anything else for five hours; monitor your body reaction for nausea, vomiting, diarrhea, faintness, or excess fatigue.

6. **Eat:** Consume small amounts at first, gradually building up if there are no adverse effects.

This might seem like a long process for each plant, but these steps could save your life. I was once advised by an "expert" that a certain heart of palm was safe to eat. I had never heard of a heart of palm that wasn't edible, so

I consumed the plant. After a few mouthfuls, my throat felt tight and my tongue was fuzzy. I ceased eating the palm and wiped my hands on my legs to get rid of the sap. Immediately, my fingerprints became raised and swollen patterns appeared on my legs. The sap had irritated my skin. If only I had followed my toxin test steps, I never would have consumed that plant and risked my life.

If you do become sick from something you have eaten, the following actions may provide you with some relief:

- Drink a lot of water if you have it to spare

- Induce vomiting

- Eat some crushed charcoal

- Mix some white wood ash to a paste with water and consume

The charcoal possesses properties that bind toxins to its particles and aid in elimination from the body. White wood ash can have an alkalizing effect on the stomach.

Don't limit yourself to certain parts of the plant. A lot of edible plants can be consumed from tip to root. Experiment with:

- Leaves and stems (the younger, the better)

- Roots and tubers

- Fruits

- Nuts (may need boiling to get out all of the tannins)

- Seeds and grains

- Flowers

- Inner bark (raw, boiled, or roasted)

- Lichen (soaked overnight and boiled thoroughly)

Although it is hard to know what will be in your specific area, there are some easily identifiable plants that are prolific around the world and are good to know and be on the lookout for.

▶ COMMON EDIBLE PLANTS

COCONUTS Found on over 65 percent of the world's coastlines, coconuts are easily identifiable and hard to confuse with any other plant. Mature, ripe coconuts contain a clear liquid that is great for hydration, and the flesh of the coconut can be consumed both from the green coconuts and the dried brown nut. Rather than climbing the tree, see if you can find a long, forked stick to knock the coconuts to the ground.

PALMS Heart of palm is the edible inner bark found in the top of the tree between where the oldest leaves begin and the youngest leaves end. The trunk is usually a darker brown color, and the indicator is a clearly defined line between there and a lighter green area where the leaves begin. Cut this area off with a knife or sharp rock, and peel off the outer layers. The super-soft white part in the center is the edible part. Make sure to run through the toxin testing steps first to see if that palm is edible for you.

BAMBOO Easily recognizable, as most species look very similar, long, straight bamboo stalks are jointed and hollow and often grow in thick stands. You can consume the young shoots found at the base of the plant. Cut them off at the base, and peel away the outer layers to expose the white inner flesh. While it is okay to eat bamboo shoots raw for a little while, it is best to boil or roast them if possible, as the raw bamboo contains traces of cyanide that can eventually lead to weakness, confusion, loss of consciousness, and death.

STINGING NETTLES This is one of those plants that goes against my rules of thumb about what to avoid. It is found alongside most rivers and creeks in temperate climates all over the world. Stinging nettles have small hairs that act as an irritant if they come in contact with skin, but these hairs are easily neutralized by scraping or boiling. Nettles are one of the most nutritious wild edibles, containing more iron than spinach and high levels of calcium, fiber, and vitamin C. It will be hard to avoid getting stung in the harvesting process, but the sap of the nettle actually provides a soothing relief from the sting. It's best to harvest the nettles when they are young and not flowering.

CATTAILS This plant can be found in wetlands all over the world. The green seed head can be consumed raw but is best boiled and eaten like corn on the cob. When the seed head is pollinating, collect the pollen, add water, and make it into dense, nutritious cakes to cook by the fire. The young shoots can be gathered, peeled, and eaten raw or boiled. The roots can be dug up and cooked like potatoes, or dried and ground down into a flour that can be used for making flatbreads or added to stews as a nutritious thickener.

SEAWEEDS If you happen to find yourself by the coast, it is good to know that there are no poisonous seaweeds. There are some that may act as a slight laxative or diuretic, but none of them will result in your death when consumed. Eating a small amount and increasing the serving over time will show you which ones may have this effect. It's best to eat seaweeds fresh rather than if they have been lying on the beach for a while, and consume them quickly or dry them for future use when you pick them, as their composition changes quite rapidly once harvested. Seaweeds can be high in iodine, so if you have a thyroid problem, it is best to consume them in small doses.

3.5.2

▶ FAUNA

As a general rule, the flesh of all land mammals is edible. This means if you can catch it and kill it, you don't have to be worried about knowing exactly what it is or subjecting it to any toxin tests.

I like to divide the animals around me into two simple groups: predators and prey. This is another version of my risk-versus-reward calculation. If something is likely to kill me, it's the predator and I'm the prey. These animals feature as a high risk compared to reward. If I can kill an animal without much danger to myself, then it is low risk, high reward. Once I have distinguished between my predators and prey, I can then look at what animal food source I have around me.

Keep in mind that in a lot of countries, harvesting certain animals is illegal either all year-round or during parts of the year without a permit. Trapping and snaring animals is also illegal in some countries, as it is an indiscriminate form of hunting. This means you can't choose the animal that your trap will catch. Know the local laws surrounding hunting and trapping, but remember that in a survival situation, these laws are waived if you have broken any of them in order to save your life.

3.5.2.1

▶ EDUCATE YOURSELF

The worst thing you can do when hunting in a survival scenario is to throw yourself into the situation without educating yourself. You risk scaring away your viable food sources (perhaps for good) and also wasting valuable time and energy on failed hunts.

Moving silently and slowly through your surroundings, listening for sounds, following game trails, and checking out prints by water sources will provide you with valuable information about what animals may be in the area. Animals tend to be creatures of habit and will often frequent the same watering holes, feeding areas, and bedding-down areas. This will enable you to learn how best to make a kill or what traps to set.

The information you are trying to gather will include:

- **What animals are in your area—size of groups and type**

- **Where they drink**

- **Where they eat**

- **Where they hang out during the day**

- **The paths they follow**

- **How aggressive they are**

- **Their strengths and weaknesses**

Most mammals move at first and last light, choosing to bed down in the heat of the day.

Signs that will help you find the animals in your area include:

TRACKS Pay careful attention to the ground around you. Mud by watering holes usually gives a clear indication of what is drinking there. Animals like to move through the bush the same way as humans do—on unobstructed paths and walkways. They will often follow the same path, leaving clear trails for you to follow. Depending on the weather and soil type, you can get a sense for when an animal last went down that path. Things to be aware of are:

- When it last rained; if the track has raindrop marks evident on it or if that track was made since the last rain.

- How windy it is; if the soil is loose or sandy, the wind will soon erase all signs, so a track could have been made very recently if it is obvious in the sand.

- If the track is dry or wet; an animal exiting water recently will leave a wet track.

To start to understand the time frame of tracks in your area and weather conditions, place an obvious footprint of your own in the ground and observe what happens to it over time.

DROPPINGS Animal scat can reveal some of the most valuable information about the animals in the area. Don't be squeamish. You will have to get in there and have a good look to find out the information you need. Droppings can tell you:

- The animal type, if you know what types of animals leave what type of droppings.

- What they eat: Is there hair in the droppings, suggesting a carnivore or omnivore, or are they mainly vegetarian? This information can also help you know what to bait traps with.

- The size of animal.

- When they were around: If the droppings are very fresh, they will have a coat of moisture or slime on them; after an hour or so, they can still be wet but flies are usually buzzing around the droppings at this stage; dry droppings are usually a day or so old, depending on your environment.

OTHER SIGNS Some animals make it obvious that they have passed by. This includes destruction to the vegetation from feeding or rubbing against it. Clawed climbing animals will leave holes and claw marks on the tree trunks. Pigs and deer will wallow and "root" around in the grass and mud, leaving dig marks with obvious hoof prints in them. Burrowing animals will test the ground for new digs, leaving scrapings with paw marks in them as well as their obvious burrow homes. Animals may also be digging for food, such as termites and ant nests. Grubs burrow into tree trunks and branches, leaving perfectly round holes as a clue to their whereabouts. Any signs of disturbance that aren't from your habitation may be a clue to what you could eat.

3.5.2.2

▶ KEEP YOUR OPTIONS OPEN

Mammals tend to be the obvious food of choice in a survival situation, since most people are used to eating them, but there are all sorts of animals that will keep you alive out there:

REPTILES

Snakes and lizards can be a great food source. Treat all snakes as if they are venomous, unless you are 100 percent certain they are not. Many venomous and nonvenomous snakes look alike, and the myth about their pupil shape is a dangerous misconception that can lead to you getting killed.

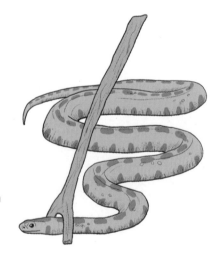

A long, forked stick is a good method of pinning down a snake. Make sure that you pin down the snake close behind its head, as they are extremely flexible and can spin back and bite you if not properly pinned. If you have a blade, cutting off the snake's head is the quickest way to dispose of the snake, but a rock to the head is as effective. Just make sure the snake is dead, not stunned, before processing it further.

A snake's fangs can retain their venom for a long time after the snake is dead; make sure you dispose of the head, fangs down, so no one will accidentally puncture themselves.

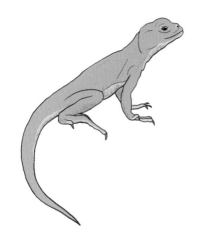

Personally, having lived off snake for quite some time in a survival scenario, I prefer the taste of the venomous snakes to the nonvenomous, but in a risk-versus-reward scenario, the nicer taste isn't worth risking your life over.

When preparing larger snakes and lizards to eat, slice them from anus upwards, and remove the guts before cooking. You can place the whole reptile on the coals, cut into pieces, and kebab, or cut into chunks and boil for a nutritious soup. Sometimes you will have the added bonus of eggs, which are usually creamy and delicious cooked on a hot rock or boiled. Smaller lizards can go straight on the fire or kebab style on sticks and don't require gutting before consumption if you cook them well.

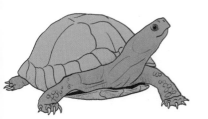

Turtles and tortoises are generally a little easier to catch than other reptiles and are not venomous, but in my experience, there isn't a lot of meat on land turtles. They tend to be mostly hollow under the shell, but if the turtle has good, chunky legs and a long fleshy neck, then it will be worth your while. The shells will make valuable pots for you to catch water in or use for storage.

Frogs are edible and easy to catch, once you get the hang of it. Some people like the grabbing-hand method, but other people prefer a thin spear with multiple prongs on the end as their frogging weapon of choice. While there is not much meat on a frog, their legs are a delicacy in some countries for a reason. If you get good at frogging, you will be able to provide a decent meal for yourself. They are best hunted at night, which makes it harder if you don't have a light source, but they will also be prevalent during and after rains, so it is worth venturing out from your shelter to take a look if you are in a swampy or tropical region. Some toads can be eaten, but they usually secrete a toxin from their skins that make them best avoided.

Avoid toads.

Toads have shorter legs and tend to have lumpy backs.

If you are unsure if what you have is a toad or a frog, the main way to tell them apart is that frogs have long legs in relation to their body and tend to jump, whereas toads have shorter legs and prefer to crawl around. Frogs also have smooth back skin, whereas toad's backs are lumpy. However, there are exceptions to this rule, so if in doubt, don't eat it. **Avoid brightly colored frogs, as they can be extremely poisonous.**

BIRDS

If you can manage to find a nesting site for birds or a place where flocks gather, you can be assured of a good meal. Bird flocks can be hard to sneak up on because there are so many eyes watching for predators, but if you can figure out a pattern on where they roost or hang out during the day, you can make your way to the area before they get there and set up a hide. A hide is merely a place of camouflage where you can sit and your prey can't tell that you are there. If you build a hide, try to build it when the birds are not in the area, and then give them a few days to get used to it before you use it. I find that throwing a heavy stick into a flock of birds is the best way to hunt them in a primitive setting. If the stick is weighted heavier on one end, it will spin into the flock and have a greater chance of hitting one and either injuring it or killing it.

If I want to preserve the feathers for further use (they can greatly contribute to warmth and comfort), I generally skin the bird as I would any mammal. The skin comes off with the feathers still attached, which makes them much more manageable, and you can gut and cook the bird over an open fire. You can also pluck the bird, gut it, and cook it. Remember, everything can be an asset to you in a survival situation, so don't throw away the feathers.

If you can find a roosting area, don't forget to check for eggs. They can be consumed raw or cooked. Don't take all the eggs. Leave some to hatch in case your survival scenario stretches into the long term.

INSECTS

Eighty percent of the world's population eats insects on a regular basis. They are a very good replenishable source of protein. If you can get your mind around using them as a food source, they can be what gets you out of your situation alive.

There are some insects to avoid as a general rule. They include:

- Caterpillars
- Grubs found on the underside of leaves
- Insects feeding on carrion or dung
- The brightly colored of any type

Go-to insects:

- **Grasshoppers, locusts, crickets, and cicadas**
These can be eaten whole, but I usually pull off the head, as the guts comes out with it, and thread the bodies on a small twig to roast over the fire. The easiest way to catch them is to swat them from a distance with a leafy branch. This stuns them and makes them much easier to catch. Be aware that if you have an allergy to shellfish, you may also have an allergy to crickets, grasshoppers, and cockroaches, so eat with care.

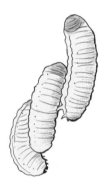

- **Grubs** These can range from small firefly larvae in the Amazon to the large wood moth larvae found in most parts of Australia. As awful as they sound to eat, grubs are a classic case of "you are what you eat." If the grubs are located inside nuts or still-living trees and roots, they tend to have a nutty flavor when eaten raw, and akin to buttery nut popcorn when eaten cooked. If the grubs are in rotten logs or dirt, they will have a woodier flavor. They are all still amazingly high in protein and a good source of fat, which can be hard to come by in a survival situation. The best way to figure out if a grub is in a tree or nut is to look for a hole. If there is one hole, the grub is generally still in there. If there are two close together, then the grub has probably hatched and left. Breaking open rotten logs is also a good way to locate them.

- **Bees** Most active during the day, bees return to the hive at night. If you locate a hive (watching the common direction bees are flying can be an indicator), then wait until it is near dusk and find a way to transport smoky fire to the entrance. This

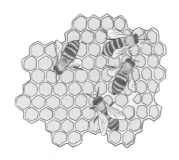

could be on water-soaked bark or in a container, if you have one. If possible, you can build a smoky fire close to the entrance of the hive. The smoke needs to be blowing into the hive to confuse the bee's pheromone production. It eventually causes them to become sleepy and pass out. You can then collect the bees, the honey, and the bee larvae. All are delicious and edible. The larvae can be eaten raw or cooked. The honey is best raw, and the bees are best cooked with the stinger removed. European bees roam as far as two miles from their hives, but Australian native bees will be no more than 500 yards from their hives when foraging. Wasps are also edible but have a small risk versus reward factor, due to their multiple sting ability and the fact they do not produce honey.

- **Termites** Usually found in mounds on the ground or in trees, or in dead wood, termites can be harvested by breaking off a chunk of the mound and shaking them free. Eat them raw or roast them in a pan. You can also eat their larvae. If you find a dead branch with termites living in it, you can put one end of the branch on the fire and catch them as they retreat from the heat. Termites are also amazing for a variety of other things. They can help you find north, as they tend to make their nests on the sunniest side of the tree. This is the north in the Southern Hemisphere and the south in the Northern Hemisphere. Regardless of the specifics of this knowledge, you can make sure that you are not going around in circles simply by making sure you keep the termite nests consistently on one side in the direction you are traveling. Crushing termites between your hands and rubbing them on your exposed skin can help deter insects, and wetting down the termite nest itself will provide you with a sticky clay that is great for making pots and bowls.

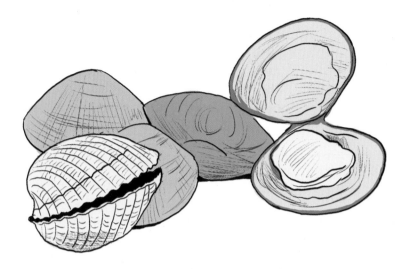

- Mollusks **In the ocean, these usually can be located between the high and low tide mark, on rocks or under the beach sand where holes or divots will give them away. Dig a foot down into the wet sand where you see those clues. You may need a sharp edge to pry them off the rocks, or just smash the outer shell and scoop it out with a sharpened twig. Avoid any mollusks that are brightly colored, and do not eat them if the following occurs:**

- They remain partially open when you touch them.

- They are easy to remove from the rocks or have fallen off by themselves.

- They smell bad.

- They don't open when cooked in boiling water.

- They are located in water with a reddish algae tinge.

With land snails and slugs, it's best to purge them for a few days in case they have been eating any vegetation that is toxic to you, so put them in a container with some fresh grass if possible. Wash them thoroughly and boil; cook them in their shells on the open fire or roast them on skewers.

Do not eat mollusks that are bright in color or shaped like cones.

One species of cone shell is one of the most venomous creatures on the planet. There are over 400 different species of cone shells, and not all of them are deadly, but most of them will deliver an envenomated barb that will range from extremely painful to life threating if it pierces your skin, so they are best avoided entirely.

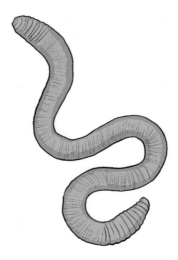

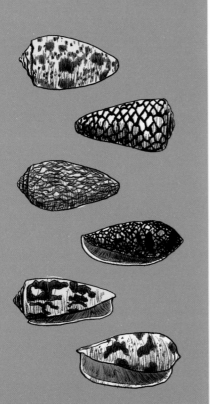

- Worms **Worms can be eaten immediately and raw but generally are quite gritty. Roasting on skewers can make them a little more palatable.**

My biggest recommendation with wild meats is to cook them well. Overcook them if in doubt. Unlike store-bought meats, wild meats can contain parasites and diseases that could make you sick if consumed raw. The best way to kill these is by boiling or roasting.

Hunting can be broken down into two different types: passive and active. Passive hunting is when you put a mechanism in place and wait for it to secure the animal for you. This includes traps and snares. Active hunting is when you are in pursuit of an animal and kill it through some force exhibited by you. This includes chasing it down on foot and using weapons.

4

First Aid

NO SURVIVAL BOOK WOULD BE COMPLETE without a section on first aid. But keep in mind that reading about how to do something is no substitute for hands-on experience in a course taught by professionals. This section is here for emergencies, or to jog your memory if you have forgotten what to do in the heat of the moment.

Recommended procedures are constantly changing, as research finds more effective ways of administering first aid in both urban and wilderness settings, so it is good to update your CPR qualifications every year and your wilderness first aid every three. They also differ from country to country, so if you are in charge of a group of people, make sure you are qualified for the country that you are working in.

I have over thirty years of first aid and wilderness first aid course experience, in three different countries. I have always kept my qualifications up to date, and I have never once learned all the same things in any course. I always learn something new, and the recommended procedures always change. I have used my knowledge often in both urban and wilderness environments. I wouldn't go so far as to say that I have saved anyone's life, but I have made them comfortable and ensured that they were in the best condition they could be once professional medical care arrived.

Your initial response to the scene of an accident will be the same regardless of whether you are in an urban or wilderness setting and if you have brought a first aid kit or not. That is the DRS ABC of being a first responder.

FIRST AID

4.1

▶ **DRS ABC**

This is a handy acronym to help you remember your order of priorities in a first aid scenario.

DANGER

The last thing that you want in an emergency scenario is to put a healthy person in danger. Once you also become a victim, chances of survival diminish. As soon as you see a person in trouble or if you come across someone who looks injured, check the area for danger. What was the mechanism of injury? Is it something that will cause injury to you? Has the danger passed, or can you safely remove the victim from danger?

If you have seen someone fall to the ground because a branch broke, it should be safe for you to move in to help them immediately. If someone has fallen because of a rockslide, wait until the slide has settled before you move in to help them.

Always take a moment to assess the scene. You may want to jump in and rescue someone from danger, but acting proactively will usually have a better result than acting impulsively. This can be seen with the amount of people who drown trying to rescue loved ones from riptides in the ocean. If they took a moment to grab a floatation device before entering the water, their success would almost be guaranteed. Diving in without one ends up putting two lives in danger.

RESPONSE

Once you have established that there is no danger to either party, it is time to assess their level of consciousness. If the person is yelling or screaming, their trachea (the body's largest airway) is clear, and they have a pulse. Move on to your secondary assessment.

If the person is still, try to get a response from them. Don't shake them violently, because you are still unsure what else may be wrong with them.

Simply touch their shoulder and say things like: "Hello," "Can you hear me?" "What's your name?" and "Can you squeeze my hand?" Give them a moment to respond. If they moan, open their eyes, or answer a question, you can move on to your secondary assessment.

If there is no response, assume they are unconscious and roll them into the recovery position. If the mechanism of injury was a fall from a height or a head hit, assume that the spine may be damaged, and take extra care when moving them into the recovery position to keep the spine straight, if possible.

THE RECOVERY POSITION

An unconscious person is placed in this position, as it allows the airways to stay open and fluids to drain out if need be. The tongue muscle may fall back and block the airways of an unconscious person on their back. To move someone into the recovery position, lie them on their back, bend the arm nearest to you so that their hand cushions their head, and bend the opposite knee to you. Pull the person over onto their side so that their knee holds them on their side. Tilt their head back slightly to ensure their airways are open.

SEND FOR HELP

This was a more recent addition to first aid teachings, because it was a step that people in urban environments kept forgetting to do. If you are with a group of people and have access to cell phone service, this is the moment when you delegate someone to call 911. If you are by yourself, take a second to dial, put the phone on speaker, and continue with your assessment.

In a wilderness environment, it can get tricky. If you have cell service, dial 911. If you don't have service where you are, continue with your assessment. It is best to get more information before you send for help.

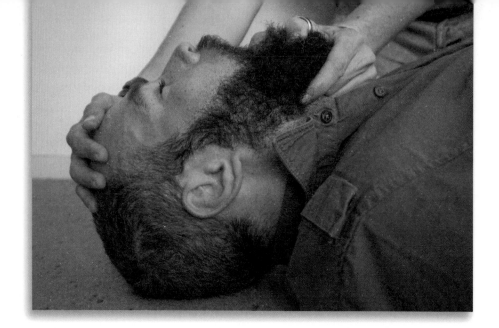

AIRWAY

Look for any obstructions in the mouth. Check and scoop out anything that you see inside their mouth that shouldn't be there. If their breathing is wheezy or noisy, there may be something blocking their airway. Do not shove your fingers too far down their throat to try to clear it out, as this will trigger the gag reflex. If you can't see anything, check their breathing.

BREATHING

If the airway is clear, check for breathing. This can be done by listening, looking, and feeling. Place the back of your hand by their mouth to see if you can feel air moving by. Place your hand high on their chest to see if you can feel a rise and fall. Listen to see if you can hear their breath moving in and out.

If the person is breathing, keep them on their side and continue to do your secondary assessment.

If the person isn't breathing, turn them onto their back and commence CPR. This would be the time I would recommend sending someone for help, if you are out of cell phone range. If you are alone with the victim, set off your personal locator beacon or stay with the patient and continue to the next step if neither of these options is available.

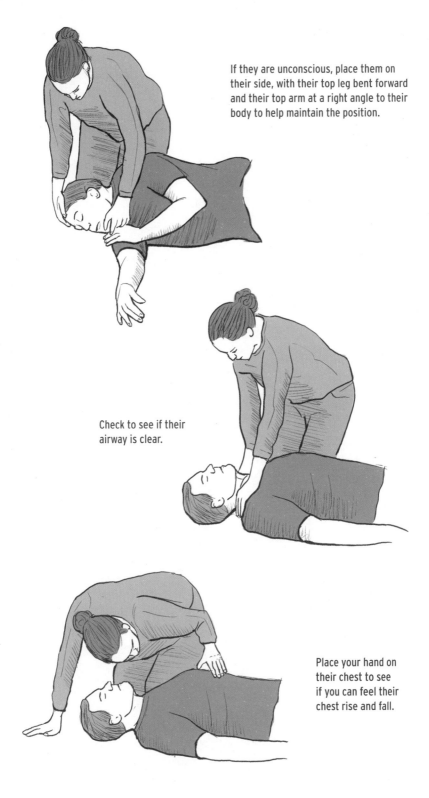

If they are unconscious, place them on their side, with their top leg bent forward and their top arm at a right angle to their body to help maintain the position.

Check to see if their airway is clear.

Place your hand on their chest to see if you can feel their chest rise and fall.

COMPRESSIONS

There are many schools of thought as to how many compressions per minute and how many rescue breaths, but as long as you are doing compressions and breaths so that blood is continuing to circulate through the body and oxygen can get to the brain, you are doing more than nothing. Thirty compressions to two breaths is considered fairly standard. In times of airborne pathogens, choosing whether or not to do rescue breaths will be up to you. If you know the person and know their health status, you may make a choice to do assisted breathing. If the patient is a stranger, it is okay to just give chest compressions, knowing that some air will be moving in and out of their lungs while you are massaging their heart.

How to do chest compressions:

- Kneel by the person's side.
- Place the heel of one hand in the center of the person's chest.
- Place the heel of your other hand on top of the first hand.
- Interlock your fingers.
- Position yourself vertically above the person's chest.
- Keep your arms straight, and press down on the sternum about three inches.
- Keep a pace of approximately one hundred compressions per minute.

How to do assisted breathing:

- Pinch the soft part of the patient's nose closed.
- Tilt their head back slightly.
- Use a pinch grip to raise up their chin.
- Take a normal breath, and place your lips around the person's lips, creating a seal.
- Blow steadily into their mouth while watching to see if the chest rises.
- Remove your mouth, and let the chest fall.
- Take another normal breath, and blow into the patient's mouth.

If the chest isn't rising when you breathe into their mouth, try tilting the head back a little more, or look for an obstruction in their airway.

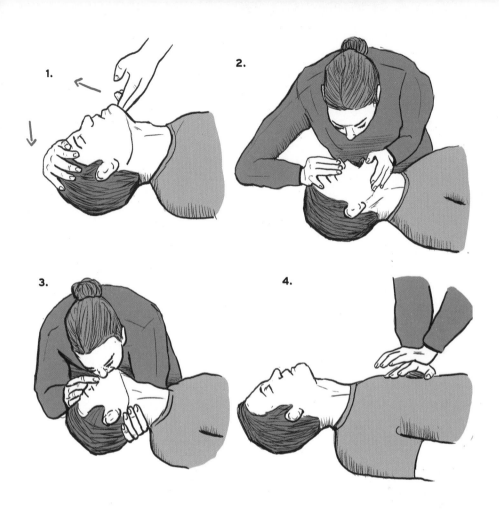

1.

2.

3.

4.

You will need to continue CPR until such time as the person is breathing on their own, a medical professional has arrived to take over, or your health and safety are compromised. You may be able to swap in and out with other people if you aren't alone, allowing for some rest between rounds.

If you are in an urban environment, there is a good chance that a defibrillator is somewhere nearby and someone has managed to access it for you. Using one of these would be the next step, if this is available and they haven't responded to the first few rounds of CPR.

A person will either recover and start breathing, or they won't. In a wilderness setting, if they recover, you will need to get this person to medical attention as soon as possible. Either get help to come to you or assess and evacuate on your own. It is important to understand that chances of resuscitation are slim without intervention from either a defibrillator or a professional medical team. Do not feel like you have failed if you are unable to resuscitate someone. The failure would have been in not possessing the knowledge to at least try.

You can manage to get through the first few minutes of a first responder incident without needing any equipment. This is why it will be similar procedures wherever you are. It is when dealing with further injuries that having a first aid kit available may be the difference between competently dealing with a situation and managing to get someone to safety, or having to improvise and risk incomplete healing or infection. Always carry a first aid kit into the outdoors, and know how to use it.

SURVIVAL FIRST AID

In a survival scenario, I will assume that you don't have a first aid kit with you and make suggestions as to some alternative things you can try. This is where you will need to get inventive and be adaptable. Think about what would solve the problem if you were in civilization, and then explore your environment to figure out what you can use that might deliver a similar result. I am also going to assume that you are unable to get help, because you would have gotten out of your survival scenario if that was an option. This is why I emphasize a risk-versus-reward analysis of every task you undertake while trying to survive. Something like a small cut that you effortlessly and routinely tend to at home can kill you if you can't keep it clean in the wilderness.

SECONDARY ASSESSMENT

If the person is conscious or unconscious but breathing, you will need to check to see what else has to be done to keep them alive. This is where the scenarios become too numerous for me to list off. There are situations that need to be dealt with immediately or the person will deteriorate, such as deadly bleeds and venomous snakebites, and situations that are not so urgent, like blisters and splinters. Generally, a conscious person will be able to describe what has happened to them, which will cut down the guesswork of what you need to treat. It will also be easier if you are around them when they became unconscious. It is only when you come across an unconscious patient that you will need to do some investigation as to the possible cause.

Be aware that immediately after an accident, a patient may be flooded with adrenaline, which might mask symptoms of whatever injury they have sustained. I love this adrenaline because it enables me to finish whatever task I'm trying to complete before dealing with the injury, but it can also mean that you may miss serious conditions in your first aid assessment.

I will discuss some of the more common scenarios that you may encounter while interacting with the outdoors and how best to deal with them. I have divided them up into injuries and illnesses.

4.2

▶ INJURIES

DEADLY BLEEDS

A severed artery can lead to someone bleeding out in minutes. It doesn't take much. I have lost count of the times I have seen people cutting something with a knife while resting the object on their leg. Fatigue and momentary lapses in concentration can have disastrous consequences when combined with sharp objects or projectiles.

Deadly bleeds are wounds where the blood is pumping from the wound, the bleeding doesn't slow down or stop with pressure, and/or the blood is quickly soaking through the bandage. Deadly bleeds can be internal or external. External ones are more obvious, as there will be blood soaking clothing or flowing from the wound. Internal bleeds can generally be observed as swelling or bruising at an impact site. If the swelling or bruising is in the abdominal region, call for help and evacuate as soon as possible.

For all deadly bleeds, immediate evacuation and medical assistance will be required. Treat the wound first before dialing emergency services, if you are alone or if it is just you and the victim. Assign someone else to dial, or head out for help immediately if you are in a group.

If the object is still in the body, do not attempt to remove it. If it is protruding from the wound, immobilize it in place so it doesn't move around and create further damage internally. Removing projectiles in the wilderness could open up arteries, and the patient can bleed out in minutes.

The first thing to do with a massive bleed is to apply pressure to the wound. Grab some absorbent material if you have any available, or use your hands to try to stem the bleeding. In some cases, wounds will stop bleeding when pressure is applied to them. Elevate the wound above the level of the heart if possible. If you have absorbent dressing and a bandage available, place the dressing on the wound and wrap it in place with a bandage. You want a firm bandage but not a tourniquet. If the wound bleeds through the dressing, do not remove the initial dressing; simply apply another layer of absorbent material and another bandage.

STRAIGHT-SIDED DEEP CUT

If the wound is a slice cut, hold the two sides of the wound together as you apply pressure. Once bleeding has slowed, flush out the wound and check the depth of the wound and whether it looks like it will continue to bleed. If the wound requires stitches, use butterfly stitches from your first aid kit to hold the sides of the wound together, and cover it with a clean nonadhesive dressing.

WOUNDED LIMB If the wound is deep and to a limb, apply pressure, elevate the area above the heart, and cover it with a pressure bandage, making sure that it is firm but not tight enough to cut off circulation to the extremities. You want a firm bandage but not a tourniquet. If the wound bleeds through the dressing, do not remove the initial dressing; simply apply another layer of absorbent material and another bandage.

ABDOMINAL WOUND If the wound is in the abdomen, and there are no internal organs visible, treat it as above. If there are internal organs visible or protruding, **do not try to stuff them back in the cavity.** Cover the wound with a moist, sterile dressing and bandage it firmly. Make the victim comfortable, but do not give them anything to eat or drink.

CHEST WOUND If the wound is in the chest and a wheezing noise can be heard through the wound, assume that a lung has been punctured. Cover the hole with a dressing to create a pressure seal. This can be a resealable plastic bag or something similar. Tape around three edges of the square, allowing one side to remain free. Immobilize until help can arrive.

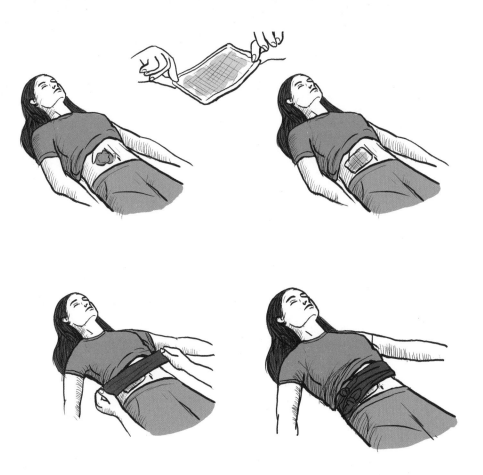

Treating an abdominal wound.

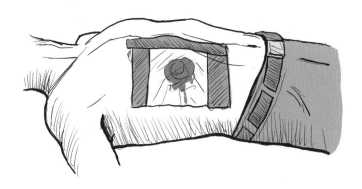

Treating a chest wound.

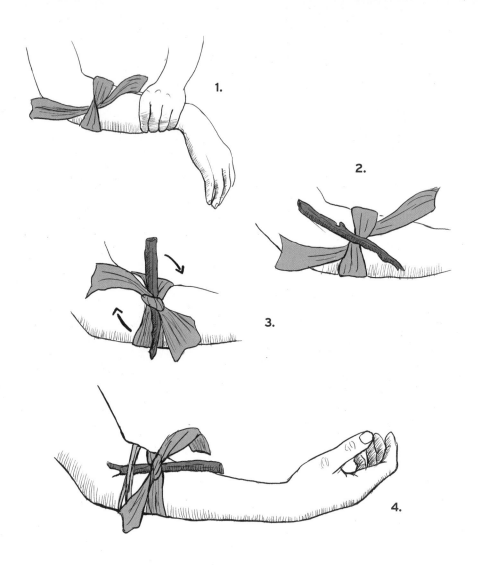

TOURNIQUET

Unless a limb has been completely shattered or torn off, or the femoral artery (the main one in your leg) has been compromised, try to avoid applying a tourniquet. A tourniquet is a last resort, as it will probably result in the loss of a limb once applied in the field. If your choice is to lose a life or lose a limb, apply a tourniquet and do not take it off. A tourniquet is a bandage that restricts all blood flow to a body part. Write the time and date that you applied it. The only person who should remove a tourniquet is a medical professional, once the person has made it to a medical facility.

SURVIVAL SCENARIO

If a deadly bleed occurs, apply pressure to the wound. If you have any spare absorbent material, place it over the wound and use whatever cordage you have to keep it firmly in place. If the bleeding stops, try to keep the wound clean by washing it out with purified water twice a day and keeping it covered.

Once you have dealt with DRS ABC and deadly bleeds, you should be able to take your time with further assessment.

BLUNT FORCE TRAUMA

This is most often associated with falls from a height in wilderness areas. If the fall was from a significant height or onto a hard surface, always suspect a spinal injury and treat it as such until the possibility can be ruled out. If the person has hit their head, treat them for a spinal injury until the possibility can be ruled out.

SPINAL INJURY

If they have an obvious head injury, immobilize them, paying attention to keeping the spine in a neutral position. Spinal injuries can present symptoms such as:

- **Extreme back pain or pressure in the head, neck, or back**

- **Weakness or paralysis in any part of the body**

- **Numbness, tingling, or loss of sensation in extremities**

- **Loss of bladder or bowel control**

Do not attempt to move someone who is displaying any of these symptoms. Call 911 if you have service, or set off your emergency beacon. If you cannot reach anyone, make the patient as comfortable as possible, and have someone head out to where they can contact emergency services. If you are the patient and you are alone, do not attempt to make your way out, as you have the potential to cause more permanent damage. Try not to panic, make yourself as visible as possible, and wait for rescue.

Immobilize and rest. Assess the injury daily and act accordingly. If you are able to heal through rest, take it slowly until there is no pain associated with movement.

Concussion: This is another serious injury caused by blunt force trauma. There is a mistaken idea that concussions only happen with a direct head hit, but landing on your feet from a high fall can also jar your cranium and result in a concussion. Signs and symptoms to look out for include:

- Confusion
- Headache
- Lack of coordination
- Memory loss
- Nausea

- Vomiting
- Dizziness
- Ringing in the ears
- Sleepiness
- Excessive fatigue

The decision to self-evacuate or wait for rescue will depend on the severity of these symptoms. Usually the treatment for a concussion is absolute rest from any physical or mental stimulation until signs and symptoms reside. You will need to assess how far you need to walk to get to safety, what the terrain is like, the time of day, and weather conditions. If you decide to evacuate, make sure you allow for the fact that the person's balance and coordination may be compromised, and carry their pack and support them through rough terrain. If you decide to stay, make sure you wake the concussed person every few hours to assess their level of consciousness. If it is deteriorating, call emergency services and evacuate immediately.

SURVIVAL SCENARIO

Concussions will generally fix themselves with rest and time. Do not try to do any physical activities for the first couple of days, and rest when you are dizzy or nauseous. If you are looking after someone with concussions, make sure you wake them every few hours for the first twenty-four hours, and keep them resting for a few days until symptoms subside.

Broken bone: It may be hard to tell the difference between a sprained joint and a broken bone. Some things to look for will be deformities, numbness, and whether the patient heard a cracking noise when the injury occurred. Sprains will usually be associated with a popping noise. Depending on which bone is broken, the patient may be able to walk out unaided, or will not be able to support their weight at all. If the patient is unable to put weight on the injured limb, take the weight off, apply a compression bandage, and have them rest in the position most comfortable to them. If you have cold water available, soak a bandanna in the water and cover the injured area with a cooling compress.

SURVIVAL SCENARIO

If the break is internal and minor, treat as for a sprain and rest, cool, and elevate. Immobilize the limb in whatever position is most comfortable for the patient, and rest until it feels better. Do not try to reset a disfigured fractured bone in the field. The sharp ends of the bone can cut vital arteries and result in a deadly bleed. Splint the limb in whatever position is most comfortable to the patient, and strap it to the body or to the other limb to immobilize it. If bone is exposed, rinse it with purified water and try to keep the wound clean and covered to prevent infection.

Twisted ankle: This can range from a slight twist, easily walked off, to more extreme tendon and ligament damage. Assess the severity of the sprain. If you are not far from your exit and the person is able to put weight on the ankle, do not remove the boot. It is acting as a compression bandage and supporting the injury. Provide some aid in the form of a walking stick or shoulder to lean on, and slowly make your way to safety. If the patient is unable to put weight on the injured foot, take the weight off, remove the boot, apply a compression bandage, and have them rest with their foot elevated. If you have cold water available, soak a bandanna in the water and cover the foot with a cooling compress.

SURVIVAL SCENARIO

Rest, cool down, and elevate. Hopefully the limb will get better on its own with rest, but add support if necessary. Crafting a pair of crutches out of tree limbs or a walking stick may help.

BITES AND STINGS

If something bites you and you get ill, it is venomous. If you bite something and you get ill, it is poisonous. This section will look at how to deal with venom.

SNAKES

When a snake strikes, usually the venom will enter the body in the lymphatic system. Lymph only moves rapidly through the body when you move your muscles. This means the first action in dealing with a snakebite is to stay calm and still. Get out of the way of the snake and away from danger, and then lie down in a comfortable position with the heart higher than the bite site, if possible. Immobilize the limb that has the bite on it. If you are close to help, do not wash the venom off the wound, as medical professionals will use this sample to help identify the antivenom they will use to treat the victim. Simply cover the wound with a nonadhesive dressing and, using a compression bandage, wrap from the bite site up to the joint above the bite and then down to the joint below the bite. The bandage should be firm but not cut off circulation. Mark on the bandage where the bite is. Call or send for help. Do not attempt to move the patient.

SURVIVAL SCENARIO

There are countless examples of Australian Indigenous people surviving snakebites from some of the deadliest snakes in the world. They would simply find a place in the shade, make sure they have access to water, and lie down to ride it out. They would either battle a fever and sickness for a few days and be able to continue on their way afterward, or they would die. Your best chance of survival without compression bandages will be to wash the bite site, drink some water, and lie down, letting your body fight the venom slowly.

ALL OTHER BITES AND STINGS

Monitor the site of the injury for changes. If you have been bitten or stung by a land insect, put a cooling compress on the more serious stings. Having an insect bite relief cream or spray in your first aid kit is a good idea.

If there are any signs or symptoms of an allergic reaction, such as swelling of the throat or wheezing, rashes, hives, or severe swelling at the bite site, take an antihistamine and look to evacuate. I carry an EpiPen for more extreme allergic reactions such as anaphylaxis, but this is generally only available from pharmacists with a prescription for people with known allergies. If you are traveling with anyone who has a known extreme allergic reaction, make sure that they bring their EpiPen and keep it at the top of their pack.

Most marine animal stings are best treated with water that is as hot as you can bear. This can be applied with a wet cloth, or the body part can be submerged in a container, depending on the size of the area affected and where the sting is located. If you are in a marine environment, it is a good idea to carry white vinegar if you know there might be jellyfish about. This will help remove the tentacles and neutralize the venom. Marine animals have some of the most toxic venom in the world, so if you have been stung in a marine environment, evacuate and seek professional medical help as soon as possible.

SURVIVAL SCENARIO

For land stings and bites, apply cold water compresses. For marine stings, use hot water compresses. For jellyfish stings, pee on the area to remove the tentacles, and then apply hot water. This is a highly debated subject, but if your urine is acidic, which it will be if you are slightly dehydrated, then urine will work. If your urine is alkaline, which happens when you are hydrated, then it won't work. Never use salt water to remove the tentacles.

Be aware that a lot of venom from marine animals works to paralyze the respiratory system, so if you are not alone, twenty-four hours of assisted breathing for the patient will allow the venom time to work its way out of their system, and they may recover.

DROWNING

If you come across someone who is drowning, get the person out of the water if you can do so safely without compromising yourself or others.

If they are unconscious, place them on their side in the recovery position. If you are able to delegate someone to contact emergency services, do so. If you are alone, call emergency services or send out a Mayday and then check to see whether the patient's airway is clear. Place your hand on their chest to see if you can feel their chest rise and fall, or the back of your hand by their mouth to see if you can feel a rush of air. If they are not breathing, turn the patient on their back and begin to do chest compressions. There are different suggestions for how many pushes to do, but at the end of the day, as long as you are doing any at all, it is better than none. You should be aiming to compress the chest by a third. This is quite a solid push on an adult and less on a teenager and child. Use both hands for an adult and large teen, and one hand for a younger teen and child. You should be aiming at doing about one hundred thrusts in a minute.

In these times of airborne viruses, medical professionals are leaving it up to you as to whether you want to do assisted breathing or not. Chest compressions will also move the lungs of the patient enough to get some oxygen circulating to the brain, if you are uncertain. If you know the patient and feel confident about their health status, pinch the patient's nostrils, tilt their head back slightly, and deliver two long, slow breaths into their mouth for every thirty chest compressions. Continue to do so until the patient starts breathing or medical help arrives.

Being a wilderness first aid scenario, it may be some time before medical help arrives. Continue to administer CPR until the patient starts breathing or until it compromises your health and safety.

Once the patient is breathing, place them into the recovery position until they are conscious. Seek medical help as soon as possible, as water in the lungs may lead to respiratory conditions even if the patient seems fine.

SURVIVAL SCENARIO

As above. If the patient recovers, advise rest and monitor for signs of respiratory infections.

CARDIAC ARREST

Cardiac arrests can come on gradually or hit quickly.

Symptoms include:

- Sudden collapse
- No pulse
- No breathing
- Loss of consciousness

Signs of an impending issue can be:

- Chest discomfort
- Shortness of breath
- Weakness
- Fast-beating, fluttering, or pounding heart

If you or your friends are experiencing any signs of a possible heart attack, stop activity immediately and assess. How far are you from your vehicle or base? What is the terrain like? How serious are the signs? If you can make your way out to medical help, take your time and get out as quickly and safely as possible. If signs are escalating and you are unable to self-evacuate, make the patient comfortable in a seated position and call for help, or head out to get help.

If the patient collapses, immediately begin the DRS ABC procedures.

SURVIVAL SCENARIO

As above. Be aware that getting a heart started in a wilderness setting is a hard task. Usually CPR is recommended until such time as a defibrillator or medical help arrives. Cease CPR if it begins to compromise your health and safety by continuing.

BURNS

Most wilderness experiences come with the idea of sitting around an open campfire at night. It is easy to forget that a pot is hot if you pick it up, or that a burning log can roll out of the fire and make contact with skin. Depending on the severity of the burn, you may need to evacuate to medical help immediately, or simply holding it under running cold water for ten minutes could ease the pain and you can continue on your trip.

The important thing to remember with burns is that the layers of skin continue to burn after the heat source is removed, so skin that is burnt requires immediate cooling, preferably under running cold water for at least ten minutes. Keep cooling the area until removing it from the water doesn't lead to an increase in pain or until it isn't providing any further relief.

Burns extending over 50 percent or more of the body are usually fatal. Call or send for emergency help, and try to submerge the patient in cool running water for at least ten minutes.

Different types of burns:

- **First degree:** These are superficial burns that are mild compared to other burns; they cause pain and reddening of the outer layer of skin.
- **Second degree:** These are partial-thickness burns that affect the outer layer and the lower layer of skin; they cause pain, redness, swelling, and blistering.
- **Third degree:** These are full-thickness burns that go through the skin layers and affect deeper tissues; they result in white or blackened, charred skin that may be numb.
- **Fourth degree:** These go deeper than third degree and can affect your muscles and bones; nerve endings are also damaged or destroyed, so there is no feeling in the burned area.

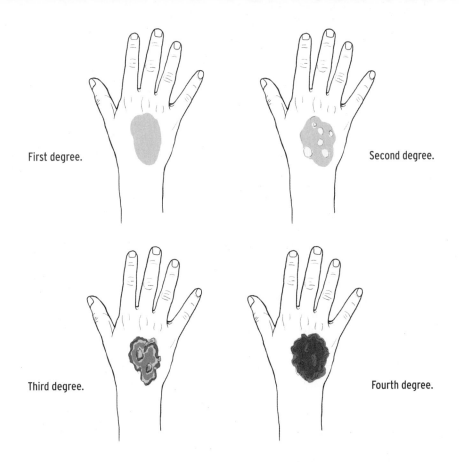

First degree.

Second degree.

Third degree.

Fourth degree.

Third- and fourth-degree burns require immediate evacuation. Cool with running water for ten minutes, and cover area with a dry, nonstick adhesive dressing. Do not apply anything else to the burn. Hydrate the patient by ensuring they continue to sip small amounts of water.

Second-degree burns will require assessment. Any burn that is larger than an inch in diameter or widespread should be cooled in running water and covered with a dry sterile dressing, and then the victim should be evacuated to medical help. If you have a burn-specific dressing or gel, it is okay to apply this if you don't have cold running water or when you are evacuating. Do not burst blisters. They are keeping the burn site sterile and reducing the chance of infection.

First-degree burns can be cooled under cold running water and monitored. Do not apply any oil-based products, as these can heat up and "cook" the area further.

SURVIVAL SCENARIO

Cool the burned area and then keep it dry and clean in order to prevent infection.

ENVIRONMENT-RELATED INJURY

These are any injuries to your body that are caused by the climate or ecosystem you are in. The treatment is the same, regardless of whether you are in a backcountry or survival scenario.

Dehydration:

- Dry mouth
- Tiredness or fatigue
- Thirst
- Headache
- Lack of urination (you should be peeing once every few hours)
- Dark-colored pee
- Dizziness

If untreated, dehydration can progress into foggy thinking, inability to make rational decisions, and eventually seizures, brain damage, and death.

Heat exhaustion This is a condition that is the result of your body over-heating. Signs and symptoms of heat exhaustion include:

- Cool, moist skin with goose bumps when in the heat
- Heavy sweating
- Faintness
- Dizziness
- Fatigue
- Weak, rapid pulse
- Low blood pressure
- Muscle cramps

The best cure for heat exhaustion is to cool the body down, so stop activity, seek shelter, and drink water if you have it. Prevention is better than having to cure it, so try not to be active in the heat of the day.

Heat stroke If heat exhaustion is untreated, it will lead to heat stroke. This is the most serious heat-related illness and occurs when the body becomes unable to control its temperature. Body temperature may rise to 106°F or higher in the space of ten to fifteen minutes. Signs and symptoms of heat stroke include:

- Throbbing headache
- Lack of sweating despite the heat
- Red, hot, and dry skin
- Nausea and vomiting
- Rapid heartbeat
- Rapid, shallow breathing
- Confusion and disorientation
- Seizures
- Unconsciousness

Cool the body down as soon as possible. Stop activity, seek shade, and use water to wet the skin while actively fanning to reduce the core temperature.

HYPOTHERMIA

This is a condition that occurs when the body loses heat faster than it can produce it. It is better to prevent hypothermia than to try to cure it in the field, so always begin to try to rewarm when you start to feel cold.

Signs and symptoms of hypothermia include:

- Shivering
- Slurred speech or mumbling
- Slow, shallow breathing
- Weak pulse
- Clumsiness or lack of coordination
- Drowsiness
- Confusion
- Loss of consciousness

Someone with hypothermia usually isn't aware of their condition, as it comes on gradually. Eventually it can lead to risk-taking behavior and a feeling of euphoria. Quite often people who have died of cold exposure are found naked, as they begin to feel overheated and take off all their clothes in the final stages of the condition.

When you start to feel cold, add layers or remove damp clothing and replace them with dry. Move around, and seek shelter and warmth. Do not attempt to warm hypothermia victims quickly, as this will lead to cold blood in the extremities rushing to the core and dropping the core temperature dangerously. Warm drinks and a hot water bottle on top of a layer of clothing by their core will help. Avoid alcohol, caffeine, and tobacco. It is not recommended to strip off and join them, because this may lead to two cold people instead of two warm people, but if you are having trouble warming them, keep your warm layers on and get close.

Frostbite This is a condition where the skin and the tissue just below the skin freeze. It mostly affects exposed body parts or extremities. Signs and symptoms include:

- Very cold flesh
- Numbness
- Hard, pale skin

To treat frostbite, rewarm slowly in tepid water and wrap. This flesh may turn black, rot, and fall off. It is important to keep the wound as clean and sterile as possible. Any flesh that has been frostbitten in the past will be more susceptible to it in the future.

Sun or snow blindness The sun reflecting off the sand or snow can amplify the glare, causing the corneas in your eyes to become "sunburnt." It can produce temporary partial or full vision loss. It is best to predict when this might happen and act proactively to prevent it. Covering sunglasses with tape to restrict light to a thin crack can help. If you don't have glasses, thin strips of bark covering the eyes will work. The idea is to restrict the amount of light entering the eyes, so whatever you have on you that will achieve that will prevent this affliction. If you have snow or sun blindness, the best thing you can do is to rest your eyes with a cold compress on them.

Altitude sickness The higher you ascend from sea level, the less oxygen is in the atmosphere. Eventually your body will feel the effects of this lack of oxygen, and you will develop altitude sickness. It happens at different heights for different people and can present in different ways.

Signs and symptoms of altitude sickness include:

- Headache
- Nausea
- Shortness of breath
- Difficulty sleeping
- Elevated heart rate
- Blue-tinged skin and nails

Eventually there can be a buildup of fluid on the brain and lungs, and this can be life threatening. Making sure that you are hydrated can help stave off altitude sickness, but unless you are carrying oxygen, the only cure for altitude sickness is to descend at once, as fast as is safe.

FOOT INJURIES

Your feet are essential in a wilderness or survival scenario. They are usually your method of transport and will allow you to do the tasks you need to do to get home or keep you alive.

BLISTERS

If left untreated, even the smallest blisters can become a life-threatening infection. They are usually caused by skin being damaged by friction or heat. The four stages of friction blisters are:

- Hot spot
- Roof intact
- Roof torn
- Deroofed

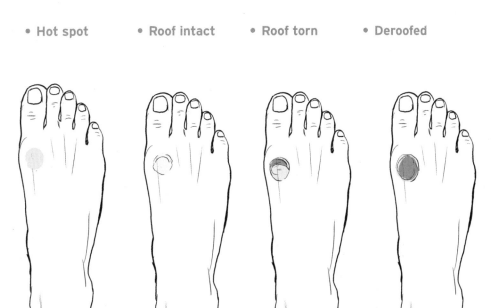

The time to deal with blisters is when they are a hot spot. Any time you have an injury that compromises a layer of skin, you are opening yourself up to the possibility of an infection, so it is best to prevent this from happening, rather than having to treat it. A hot spot is exactly as it sounds: a hot spot that begins due to rubbing. As soon as a hot spot forms, stop doing the activity that is causing it and deal with it, as it doesn't take long for a blister to form after that. Cover the area that is hot with a Band-Aid or piece of tape and continue.

If a blister has formed but is small, cover it with a Band-Aid. If the blister is large, you will need to make a donut bandage to take the pressure off it. Whatever you do, don't pop the blister, as the fluid-filled blister is keeping the skin underneath clean, which will promote healing and prevent infection.

If the roof of the blister is torn or completely gone, clean and disinfect the area and cover it with a Band-Aid. Your feet are prone to bacteria and infections from being in dirty, sweaty socks, so change the dressing and clean the blister often. If the clear fluid becomes creamy and yellow, or the area around becomes raised and red, it has become infected, and you will need to take extra care of the area and plan to hike out.

Wearing good, clean, thick woolen socks can help prevent blisters, as can the double-sock method. This is where you wear a very thin inner sock under your thicker hiking sock. This allows the material of the socks to rub against each other, rather than on your skin.

SURVIVAL SCENARIO

Keep the blistered area dry and clean. Try to avoid breaking the skin.

TRENCH FOOT

This occurs when your feet are constantly damp from sweat or submerged in water. If you don't find a way to dry your feet, the constant moisture will rot the tissue of your feet, and they will become painful to walk on and subject to infection. Dry out boots and socks at night or during the day when you are resting. Make sure you carry a spare pair of dry socks.

Find ways to get your feet out of the water, and keep them dry as much as possible.

POISONS

A poison is anything you consume that is toxic to your system. If you know that you have consumed a poison, immediately try to vomit it up. This can be done by putting your fingers down your throat to trigger your gag reflex.

Poisons will generally produce an eliminating effect on your body, which will include vomiting and diarrhea. Combat the dehydrating effects of these by consuming as much water as you can keep down. First aid kits may contain hydration salts or electrolytes that can be added to your water to help replace essential salts that your body is expelling. It is important that your body passes the poison out of its system, so try to avoid any tablets that prevent the vomiting or diarrhea for the first few hours, and only take them if you need to travel or the expulsion of fluids isn't slowing down.

Ground-up charcoal can also help bind the toxins in your stomach and pass them through your system, so the minute you begin to feel nauseous, mix some with water and drink it down.

SURVIVAL SCENARIO

Try to vomit up the poison if possible. Drink water mixed with ground charcoal and/or white ash paste; keep hydrated.

SHOCK

This is a life-threatening condition that occurs when the body is not getting enough blood flow. There are many different medical emergencies that can trigger shock. They include:

- Heart problems
- Deadly bleeds
- Allergic reactions
- Poisons
- Infections
- Damage to the nervous system

It is important to know what the signs and symptoms of shock are, because one in five people who experience shock will die from it. Signs and symptoms include:

- Anxiety or agitation
- Bluish lips and fingernails
- Chest pain
- Confusion
- Dizziness or light-headedness

- Pale, cool, clammy skin
- Profuse sweating
- Rapid, weak pulse
- Shallow breathing
- Feeling faint
- Unconsciousness

Follow the DRS ABC (see page 256), and then, if the person is conscious and responding, have the patient lie on their back with their legs slightly raised, unless some other injury prevents this. Monitor every five minutes for a change in their condition. You will need to call emergency services to arrange for an evacuation if you suspect a person is in shock, as their condition can deteriorate rapidly.

SURVIVAL SCENARIO

Follow the DRS ABC, and then, if the person is conscious and responding, have them lie on their back with their legs slightly raised unless some other injury prevents this. Monitor every five minutes for a change in their condition, and treat accordingly. Rest until all symptoms have ceased, and then take it easy for a few days.

▶ FIRST AID KITS

A first aid kit should be an essential on every trip into the outdoors and top on your list when packing your go bag (see page 22). I take a smaller first aid kit on personal day trips and a more extensive kit if I am doing a multi-day trip or leading expeditions. My kit also changes depending on where I am traveling and what sort of conditions I may face.

A first aid kit is designed to deliver the first line of aid in a medical emergency, supposing that you will be able to hand over to medical professionals if need be. This may not always be the case with wilderness first aid scenarios, and so I do carry a few things that will help me through if it takes a little longer to get to professional care.

Simply buying a first aid kit is not enough, though. You need to be thoroughly familiar with what your kit contains and how to use all the kit's contents. In the ultimate test of whether or not I am prepared, I have grabbed my first aid kit out of my car, and I will go through everything to see if I have all I should. I will also let you know why I have chosen to carry each item.

My first aid kit is red and clearly marked as a first aid kit. On the outside, it has a clear window detailing the DRS ABC steps, in case I forget them in an emergency (see page 256). Everything is clearly labeled as to what each pouch and pocket contains. It includes:

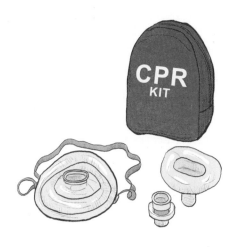

- **CPR kit:** including a hygienic face covering to allow for safe emergency breaths, and a pair of gloves

- **Major wound dressing:** which has a thick, absorbent pad attached to a bandage, ready to place and apply pressure on a deadly wound

- **2 triangular bandages:** to create slings, help apply pressure, and aid in head bandaging; they can also be soaked in cold water and used for a cold compress

- **2 pressure bandages** (usually my kit contains only one, but living and traveling in the Outback of Australia, I want a backup in case of snakebites)

- **Roller bandage:** probably don't need the extra, but it is smaller and better for sprains and strains than my large pressure bandages

- **6 safety pins:** to fasten slings or bandages

- **Hypoallergenic sports tape:** to provide support for injuries

- **6 small conforming bandages:** to keep dressings in place

- **10 nonadherent wound dressings:** for burns and abrasions

- **Combine dressings:** for major wounds

- **5 cotton gauze swabs:** for wound cleaning

- **Butterfly sutures:** for closing wounds

- **Adhesive dressings:** for minor scrapes, cuts, and blisters

- **Blister kit:** including moleskin and thin foam for making donut dressings

- **Antiseptic wipes:** to clean minor wounds and scrapes

- **Hydro gel:** for cooling down burns and scalds if I don't have access to cold running water

- **Ice pack:** for applying to sprains or breaks, or to help cool down burns and scalds if I don't have access to cold running water

- **4 eye pads:** for eye injuries
- **2 saline solutions:** for washing wounds or irrigating eyes
- **9 skin-cleaning wipes:** for cleaning dirt or blood from around a wound
- **4 sets of plastic gloves:** to prevent the exchange of bodily fluids and to keep the injury site as clean as possible

- **Emergency blanket:** for cold exposure
- **Tweezers:** for removing small, embedded objects
- **Fever strips:** to test temperature

- **Hydrolyte:** to aid in rehydration
- **EpiPen:** in case of a severe anaphylactic shock
- **Thermometer**
- **Splinter probes**
- **Hand sanitizer**

- **Sanitary items:** in case anyone in my group needs them unexpectedly
- **Pain medication:** ibuprofen to help manage pain if I am on my own and need to get back to help
- **Lip balm:** handy, but purely a comfort item
- **Pen and paper:** to record all vital information in case of an emergency

Make sure to include any prescription medication that you require.

This is a large, well-stocked wilderness first aid kit for an expedition leader. I want to make sure that I am fully able to take care of whatever emergency arises, to the best of my ability and for the long term if required. Add or take away any items you wish, but I would take a minimum of the following:

- Pressure bandages x 2
- Roller bandage
- Triangular bandage
- Gauze or cotton pads
- Strapping tape
- Adhesive dressings
- Antiseptic wipes
- Pain relief

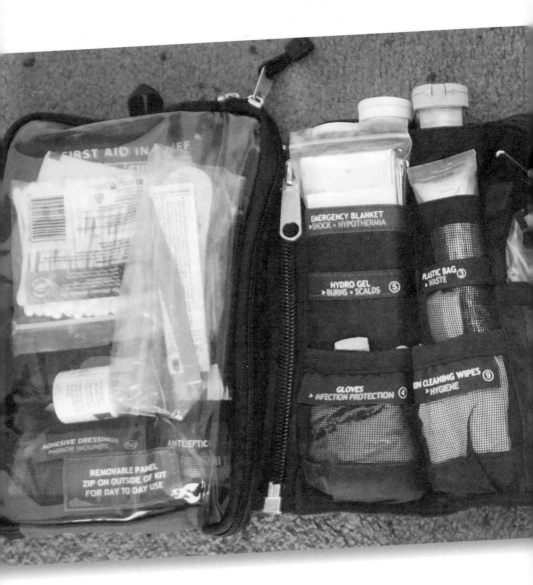